Perfect Enough

ACHIEVING HAPPINESS
AND BALANCE WITH

THE DISCOVER PROCESS

LAURA KING

1375 N. Killian Drive
Lake Park, FL 33403
877.482.7352
www.summitpress.net

To buy books in quantity for
corporate use or incentives,
call (877) 482-7352 or email
laurakinginfo@gmail.com

Credits:
Layout: Jonathan Gullery / RJ Communications
Cover Design: Timothy J. Paul * Highlan Design *
highlandesign@yahoo.com
Photographer: Allan Carlisle Photography

International Standard Book Number (ISBN) 978-0-9792996-0-5
Library of Congress Control Number: 2007929431

Printed in the United States of America

1st printing
2nd printing 2009

In loving memory of my mother,
who gave me support, encouragement,
and understanding my whole life.
I love and miss you.

SPECIAL NOTE FROM LAURA:

per·fect   (pûr'fĭkt)
adj.
1. Lacking nothing essential to the whole; complete of its nature or kind.
2. Being without defect or blemish: *a perfect specimen.*
3. Complete; thorough; utter: *a perfect fool.*
4. Excellent and delightful in all respects: *a perfect day.*

American Heritage Dictionary

e·nough   (ĭ'nʌf)
adj.
1. adequate for the want or need; sufficient for the purpose or to satisfy desire: *enough water; noise enough to wake the dead.*
    -pronoun
2. an adequate quantity or number; sufficiency
    -adverb
3. in a quantity or degree that answers a purpose or satisfies a need or desire; sufficiently.
4. fully or quite: *ready enough.*

Dictionary.com Unabridged (v 1.1)

Once you read the descriptions to the title of the book, I want you think for a moment about what it is that you really think about yourself. Are you always wanting something else or to be something different? When I decided on the title and put the puzzle pieces together for the book to take shape I begin talking to friends, clients and frankly anyone who would listen. Everyone liked the idea of being able to find that ability to be Perfect Enough. So by definition I would look to be, *lacking nothing essential to the whole; complete of its nature or kind, as a person sufficient for the purpose.* This doesn't mean that you need to shut off growth and improvement but it does mean that to become the Best You Can Be you must like you now!

SO PLEASE GIVE YOURSELF A GIFT AND OPEN YOUR MIND TO LEARN THE POSSIBILITIES.

CONTENTS

Acknowledgments 7

Foreword 9

Introduction 11

Part 1: The Tools 17

Chapter 1: What is hypnosis, and why do you need it? 19

Chapter 2: What is Neuro-Linguistic Programming,
and why do you need it? 63

Chapter 3: The Laws of the Universe and
the Natural Laws of the Mind 81

Part 2: The 8 Keys to Discover 97

Chapter 4: Self-Confidence
From Insecure to Empowered 99

Chapter 5: Self-Talk
From Denigrating to Elevating 119

Chapter 6: Persistence
From Hesitation to Determination 141

Chapter 7: Life and Aliveness
From Lifelessness to Vitality 159

Chapter 8: Health
From Illness to Wellness 175

Chapter 9: Love
From Worthless to Valuable 195

Chapter 10: Prosperity
From Scarcity to Abundance 209

Chapter 11: Meaning
From Insignificance to Purpose 227

A Final Word 242

References 245

ACKNOWLEDGMENTS

T HE MOST IMPORTANT ELEMENT about this book is the deep determination that I had to get it written—against so many odds. I had this driving force—this powerful intention—that wouldn't be stopped until I completed Perfect Enough and its companion book. Though I'm not a religious person, I am a spiritual one, and I'm certain that my intention for Perfect Enough was fueled by God. Otherwise, there's no way I would be writing this today, because there's no way I would have finished.

Everything has been presented to me in ways I cannot explain, yet I somehow knew it was all the way it should be and I trusted what was happening. And when I gave it to others to test it out, I received confirmation that the information in this book helps people manifest the results they want in life. Just like me, they trusted that they would get the results they were supposed to get and learn the lessons they needed to learn.

I want to thank my husband Ed, for being so supportive of me and my drive to get this done. He works an enormous amount of hours, but fortunately they fit in with my schedule, so we are never apart for long. The long days he works have produced character and success, and I feel blessed in that my life with him is awesome. I have a wonderful mother, brother, and sister, too, and two beautiful children, Larissa and Edward. My life is truly charmed and I'm grateful for my family everyday.

I must thank my friends: the SOS group—Regina, Cheryl, Nancy, and Lili for their faith and help in making this all work. As I sit and want to thank everyone— the list is long, but it must include Angela, for always listening to me and pushing me forward and believing in me. A special thanks to Bethany and Lisa for making sure the name Perfect Enough was created. Finally, a very special thank you to someone who has always been there and always given me a kick in the rear to keep up the pace to get this book written, Mary Martin, one of the most wonderful people I have ever met.

Many friends and clients have written to tell me of their successes after using the process we co-create for them to manifest their goals. Every e-mail and call and *thank you* and gift of appreciation makes me realize I have a gift that is not mine to own, but mine to share. This book is my way of sharing it with you.

I have written in these pages the secret for you
to have a wonderful, Perfect Enough life. Everyday holds in it
something for you to choose to enjoy.

FOREWORD

SINGLE. IN DEBT. UNHAPPY. Overweight. On the day I met Laura Boynton King, I was about to quit a job I loved but couldn't handle the stress. In one hour, Laura helped me to see the right direction. We put a "screen door" between the job I loved and the issues that were making me crazy. We put the words *money, value, worth,* and *saving,* into my mental vocabulary. And suddenly, money started filling my pocketbook.

We put cheerfulness back where unhappy had moved in. We put food back into its place of nutrition instead of feeding all my emotions. We cleaned out the regrets, the anger, the ugly and replaced that space with possibilities - beautiful possibilities. We put balance in where there was none. We moved from "never gonna get it" to "one moment please" to "done!"

Overnight, I felt and looked better. Good things started to happen. Little things, then big things. Doors opened. Possibilities became done deals. Done deals were paid. Out of debt. Happy. Slimmer - guess what happened next? Yes, the man appeared and I noticed him. I was ready to share when he arrived.

Now, I continue to use the techniques Laura has helped me and my brain develop. I'm cautious about the words that go in my brain unfiltered - and the ones I use towards others. I love stronger now as I am stronger. And I enjoy each day for the gift it is. I breathe deeper and appreciate more. My friends see the difference. My family sees the joy and I see the future - and it's bright.

Dare to take Laura's challenge. Dare to live a better life. You won't regret it. One person can change the world. Start with your world, and be the person to change it. Your path is in this book!

Lisa Anne Silhanek

Owner, Silcomm. (Silhanek Communications)

New York City, January 2007

Client of LBK since 2002

INTRODUCTION

HELLO, MY NAME IS Laura King and I'm a Certified Hypnotist, a Certified Sports Hypnotist, a Life Coach, I have my Master's Practitioner certification in Neuro-Linguistic Psychology, and I'm the founder of Summit Hypnosis Centers in Wellington, and Palm Beach Gardens, Florida.

I began studying hypnosis over thirty years ago to deal with traumatic events in my own life that left me feeling so depressed I considered suicide. After only a couple of sessions my life began to change and I didn't even know why at the time. Now I realize that what changed was my view of how much power I have to direct my life. Before that, the thought that I could direct my life didn't even occur to me; I viewed my life as something that *happened to me.*

I developed a passion to bring the benefits I received to my friends and family, and that circle quickly widened to include anyone who wanted to better their life and become who they were destined to be. I developed what I call the **DISCOVER PROCESS**, and my wish for you is that it helps you as much as it has helped my clients and me.

WHAT MAKES THE *DISCOVER PROCESS* UNIQUE?

For many people, once they realize that they need some help to get over their past mistakes and achieve what they are capable of, they go to a seminar and/or order some self-help tapes. They jump up and down, clap, and cheer enthusiastically at the seminar, then listen to the tapes every day for a week or two. Soon the excitement of their personal potential wears off and, well, they're back to where they started.

Why? Because something is missing in their approach. Reading books and seeking companionship while going through a transformational process are two ways to improve your life. However, they can only go so far because they both occur on the conscious level, and as you'll soon learn, that part of your mind is tiny in comparison to your subconscious. And the subconscious is accessed through hypnosis.

Hypnosis is a proven, time-tested way to help you achieve your goals. It has nothing to do with spirituality of any kind or the New Age movement; it's simply the utilization of the science of the mind. And it is activated by relaxation, and relaxation only. Millions of people have benefited from its power to help them make positive changes in their lives, including notables such as: Tiger Woods, Albert Einstein, Jacqueline Kennedy-Onassis, Henry Ford, Muhammad Ali, Kevin Costner, and Wolfgang Amadeus Mozart.

Hypnosis can help you transform bad habits such as smoking, eating unhealthy foods, or biting your fingernails, into good ones like saying thank you, exercising, taking better care of yourself and being more aware of what you need to do for yourself. It can help you turn your negative or sad feelings into positive, happy ones. It can help you effortlessly focus on almost anything in your life that you would like to change, while leaving you unburdened by analytical or pessimistic thoughts.

Hypnosis will help you get more out of your *DISCOVER PROCESS* because you'll be better able to let go of the negative programming from your past and create the life you want. You can rid yourself of your fears, concentrate better, discover your intentions, and believe in yourself so you can live your life at a peak level. You will eliminate any mental or subconscious barriers in order to easily gain mastery of your life.

You'll probably find that hypnosis does more than help you have a better outlook and a better ability to: cope with challenges at the office or with your family; cope with changes in your life; and balance your life. The most important gift of hypnosis is it helps you understand yourself better. In fact, it helps you *DISCOVER* your real self. When you start to relax, the things you do to prevent you from being authentic fall away, and what's left is your core being. Your internal chatter of critiquing, criticizing, and comparing yourself with a notion of perfection that doesn't exist ceases, and you become comfortable with who you really are and who you can become.

My guess is that if you're reading this book, you're a person who wants life to be more balanced and you want to learn how to have a happy and satisfying life full of peak experiences. You want to embrace and reap the benefits from knowing that you are Perfect Enough. This book, with or without the CDs, will start you (or further your progress) on a journey to the place inside your mind that can create any experience—any future—you desire, one thought at a time.

The text of Perfect Enough educates your conscious mind, and self-hypnosis helps you retrain your unconscious mind to make change. I organized the text the same way I organize my seminars. In Part I, I explain the tools I use: Hypnosis, Neuro-Linguistic Programming (NLP), and the Natural Laws of the Mind and the Laws of the Universe. In Part II, I show you how to create thoughts and actions that support your optimal self-image by using the 8 Keys of the *DISCOVER*

PROCESS. To further compound the effects of your desires, you'll create a DISCOVER board with images of your goals, and create a visualization and affirmation for the outcomes you'd like to achieve.

Each of the chapters of this book targets a critical area of your subconscious mind to create quick, easy, effortless positive change. And to illustrate how well the **DISCOVER PROCESS** works, I've included stories from my life and the lives of my clients.

> In addition, the "Perfect Enough CD Package: 8 Keys to the **DISCOVER PROCESS**" allows you to experience the benefits of hypnosis in the privacy and comfort of your home, as they allow you to achieve a level of relaxation that is difficult to reach without help. The more relaxed and confident you are, the more you enjoy what you're doing. And the more you enjoy life, the more successful you become.

HOW AM I PERFECT ENOUGH IF I NEED TO CHANGE WHAT I'M DOING?

> Because in order for anyone to embark on a journey of transformation, they must first accept themselves as being worthy, valuable, lovable, and Perfect Enough at every moment. If you think you are broken or wrong or defective, your mind will never tell you that you have the ability to improve your life, *because you are broken*. Any attempts at improvement in such a circumstance are doomed to failure.

HOW TO USE THIS BOOK

Part I of Perfect Enough gives you an overview of the essential tools necessary to realize you already are who you need to be at this moment. These tools: hypnosis, Neuro-Linguistic Programming (NLP), the Natural Laws of the Mind and the Laws of the Universe, are at the core of the effectiveness of what I do with my clients.

Chapters One and Two introduce you to hypnosis and NLP, but are by no means thorough explanations of either. If that's something you desire, any bookstore, and of course the Internet, will have oodles of information and books on both subjects, as they are both well researched and well documented. My purpose is to briefly explain why they work so well. Chapter Three explains what have been called the Natural Laws of the Mind and the Laws of the Universe. They come from various philosophical traditions and disciplines, and they are not exhaustive. They are the kernels of wisdom that guide me in my practice.

Part II: The 8 Keys to the *DISCOVER PROCESS* allows you to create a customized plan for improving your life in six months. The 8 Keys are:

1. Self-confidence
2. Self-talk
3. Persistence
4. Life and Aliveness
5. Health
6. Love
7. Prosperity
8. Meaning

For each Key, I'll guide you through the *DISCOVER PROCESS*. If you're working with the Perfect Enough Companion Book, you'll have plenty of space to make notes about your thoughts and feelings as you go through the process. If you are working with this book alone, you might want to use a notebook or journal to record your experience.

Let's use Prosperity as an example of what occurs in the *DISCOVER PROCESS*:

D = Decide that your level of prosperity is in need of enhancing.

I = Identify the fears you have that get in the way of your prosperity.

S = Self-inquiry. Here, you'll write a biography for each of your fears regarding your lack of prosperity.

C = Conscious-level action steps to improve your prosperity, such as modeling.

O = Outcome board exercise, where you paste images and words that represent your optimal idea of prosperity onto either a poster, or the board that comes with your Perfect Enough Toolkit.

V = Visualize your increasing prosperity by using your subconscious, either by reading or recording your own voice, or by listening to mine on the Perfect Enough CDs.

E = Evaluate your progress after six months.

R = Revise and repeat your affirmations

Enjoy your journey, and remember that a happy and balanced life is just a thought away.

Laura King
Palm Beach Gardens, Florida
June, 2007

PART 1
THE TOOLS

CHAPTER 1

WHAT IS HYPNOSIS, AND WHY DO YOU NEED IT?

*It is indeed unfortunate that most people hypnotize themselves
into getting the things they don't want instead of into
getting the things they do want.*
—Zig Ziglar, *See You at the Top* (Pelican 1990), p. 290

Hypnosis has had an interesting history and evokes varying images and feelings. Some people imagine a man in a theater making people quack like ducks, some think a hypnotist can make them reveal all their secrets, and some think it's all a bunch of malarkey.

The truth is that hypnosis can help you understand who you are now, and help you discover who you want to become. Best of all, once you discover who you want to be, it can help you become that person. It can help you change your bad habits into good ones and transform your negative feelings into positive ones, and it can produce these changes effortlessly.

And contrary to popular belief, when hypnosis is used for therapeutic purposes (as opposed to a stage show) you're aware and in control the entire time. If you are seeking hypnotherapy as a way to improve your life, your hypnotist has no magical power and cannot control you or make you do things you don't want to do. Hypnosis is a completely voluntary act wherein you always remain conscious; you're always aware and able to hear, to talk, and to make decisions.

So you're not going to make me quack like a duck?

Not unless that's what you want to do. I'm here to help you transform yourself into someone who is more intuitive, more effective, healthier, and more successful.

How do I know it'll work for me?

Anyone of normal intelligence can be hypnotized and you can only be hypnotized if you want to be and you willingly follow the hypnotist's instructions. There are definitely people who are more or less hypnotizable than others, and also more or less willing than others. But most people fall somewhere in the middle once they understand what it's about and realize that it's safe and it's going to help them. They comfortably go into a state of relaxation and hypnosis and are receptive to the suggestions of the hypnotist.

Think of your hypnotist as a facilitator. If you choose to follow your hypnotist's instructions, you'll be guided into a wonderful, relaxed state of focus and awareness. And afterwards, you'll remember everything that happened. All hypnosis is self-hypnosis, and all hypnosis is just relaxation.

Do you wave a pocket watch and say things like, "You are getting sleepy"?

Actually, the pocket watch is used by many hypnotherapists, but I choose to use my voice as my only tool. The sound of my voice has always worked flawlessly for me in getting my clients into a state of hypnosis. I use the induction technique of Dave Elman, which I'll describe more in a bit.

How do I know I've really been hypnotized?

At the time, you probably won't think you were hypnotized at all. Most people realize that they were indeed hypnotized after they've realize how relaxed they are and after they've seen the desired changes in their behavior. If you're using the CDs, after you've heard my voice several times, eventually just the sound of it will hypnotize you. If you were in my office, I'd know that you were hypnotized because you would give me three signs: 1) your eyelids would flutter (REM); 2) your breath would slow; 3) the whites of your eyes would get red or pink. To validate that I was correct, I'd ask you to: 1) clasp your hands tightly together, then tell you that you would not be able to separate them because they have been glued together, and that the harder you try to separate them, the more bonded they become. Then I'd ask you to try to separate them (you won't be able to); or 2) close your eyes, then I'll tell you that your eyelids are so heavy that you will not be able to open them. The harder you try, the heavier they get. Then I'll ask you to try to open them (you won't be able to).

What will I feel like when I'm being hypnotized?

I can't say for sure, because we're all unique and respond to stimulus in our own unique ways. Some people tell me they don't feel any different. Others tell me that they feel very relaxed and heavy, like a lead weight. And then there are the lucky ones who feel like they are floating on a cloud and they feel better than ever before.

How is hypnosis different from meditation?

The goal of hypnosis is to change behavior through direct suggestion and the reprogramming of the brain. Though there are myriad different types of meditation, their goal is the quieting of the mind, the concentration on a specific state (e.g., compassion, forgiveness, love, death), or the relaxation of the entire being. Though a change in your mental (or even physical) state is involved, the goal, per se, is not to alter your behavior.

HOW IS HYPNOSIS DIFFERENT FROM THERAPY?

Assuming there's no hypnosis involved, therapy appeals only to the conscious mind. It enlists the help of the intellect to solve problems and relieve stress. When you appeal to the conscious mind you can undoubtedly gain a lot of knowledge. But the more reasoning and intellectualizing you engage in, the greater the tendency to rationalize, to develop alibis, and to prevent the subconscious from changing your behavior.

WHAT IF I GET STUCK IN HYPNOSIS AND CAN'T GET OUT?

You can never get stuck in hypnosis because you have the power to emerge yourself at any time. All you have to do is tell yourself that you are emerging. All hypnosis is really just self-hypnosis. You're always in charge.

WHY DO I NEED HYPNOSIS?

When you're in a hypnotic state you can easily make positive changes because your subconscious mind is more open to suggestions for change. To understand why and how that's so, it's important to understand some things about how your mind works.

BUT FIRST, SOME FACTS ABOUT
THE HISTORY OF HYPNOSIS . . .

- Hypnosis is older than recorded history. Thousands of years ago, primitive people in Africa and Australia used chanting, drums, and the fixation of their eyes to achieve the state we now know as hypnosis. They were able to effortlessly perform amazing physical feats and easily endure situations that would ordinarily cause excruciating physical pain.

- For 200 years scientists, physicians, surgeons, theorists and researchers have been using and studying what we now call hypnosis.

- What we now call hypnosis originated with an 18th century Austrian healer named Franz Anton Mesmer (1734-1815), who hypothesized that the magnetic pull of the heavenly bodies influence the human body. This theory was called animal magnetism, and later, *mesmerism*, and his methods were theatrical and profoundly unconventional. (For example, the venue for his treatments was a darkened hall where the patient was virtually submerged in an oak tub filled with water, and objects such as broken glass, iron filings, and empty bottles were placed in the tub. The tub's cover was pierced with iron rods, which the patient would wave over the diseased parts of their body.) Though Mesmer produced astounding results and healed many people without medicine or surgery, mesmerism was widely criticized. Mesmer was soon associated with the occult and accused of flagrant charlatanism, as his experiments blended astrology and metaphysics in a way that was not appreciated at the time. (His thesis at Vienna University, where he studied theology and medicine, was entitled, "The Influence of the Planets on the Human Body.") He didn't get the approval of the scientific community, but his efforts were not for naught. None other than Benjamin Franklin, the American Ambassador in France at the time, was on the committee that investigated him, and Franklin thought Mesmer's claims and abilities were worthy of further consideration.

- In the early 1800's several pioneering Frenchmen continued investigating and experimenting with mesmerism. Eventually, in 1843, it was a well-respected English surgeon named James Braid (1795-1860) who used the term "hypnotism" and differentiated it from mesmerism. Braid demonstrated that hypnosis was a state that could be easily induced by the fixing of the patient's eyes on a single object.

- Hypnosis was successfully used as anesthesia for thousands of operations before chloroform and ether were discovered and later (and very slowly) accepted for use during surgery.

- Hypnotism was widely used by physicians and psychologists during World War I and World War II to treat battle fatigue and mental disorders resulting from war.

- The British Medical Association and the Council on Mental Health of the American Medical Association have unanimously endorsed hypnosis.

- Hypnosis is now frequently used in medicine, dentistry and psychotherapy. It is used as a part of the treatment of psychiatric/ psychological disorders, the effects of incest, rape and physical abuse, allergies, anxiety and stress management, asthma, bed-wetting, depression, sports and athletic performance, excessive self-consciousness, smoking cessation, obesity and weight control, sleep disorders, high blood pressure, sexual dysfunctions, concentration, and test anxiety.

MODERN HYPNOSIS

By far, the most influential figure in modern hypnosis is *thought* to be Dr. Milton H. Erickson (1901-1980), the founding president of the American Society of Clinical Hypnosis, who had degrees in both medicine and psychology. Erickson used myriad verbal stratagems and guided imageries to help his patients access their inner abilities to heal themselves and optimize their performance in many areas of their lives. One of the most profound of Erickson's contributions was that the subconscious can be indirectly accessed to promote healing. In other words, when he was hypnotizing his patients, he didn't tell them what they were feeling (e.g., you are getting sleepy"). Instead, he suggested to them that they *might consider* feeling a certain way (e.g., "perhaps you might notice that you are feeling sleepy"). Milton was able to put someone into a deep trance in a short period of time without mentioning the word "hypnosis" at all.

This might not seem to be a big difference but it is; it puts the patient in a position of personal control and freedom. They have their free will and can choose whether to, for instance, get sleepy. When we feel a sense of control, relaxing and accessing the subconscious is easier and more likely to occur.

Erickson also pioneered the use of verbal strategies that are very closely related to Neuro-Linguistic Programming (NLP-to be discussed in the next chapter). He realized that the way the mind processes certain words, combinations of words, words with multiple meanings, and even pauses and longer silences, profoundly affects what the mind thinks and what the body does. This will become clear in the next chapter, but for now, understand that Erickson demonstrated that language is a profoundly persuasive tool. It can engender positive change/negative change, it can increase/decrease performance, it can increase/decrease physical and mental pain, and it can even help an individual consciously control bodily functions that are usually not under our control (e.g., heart rate).

Erickson was at the forefront of clinical study and research demonstrating that the subconscious can be responsible for many of our psychological problems and much of our dysfunctional behavior. He amassed a group of zealous followers dedicated to furthering his work, and when he passed away in 1980 those followers started schools of applied psychology based on his work.

As we'll see in the next chapter, Neuro-Linguistic Programming (NLP) is one of the schools of applied psychology influenced by the Ericksonian model of hypnosis and hypnotherapy.

GIVING CREDIT TO DAVE ELMAN

At the beginning of this section, I stated that Erickson is thought to be the most influential figure in modern hypnosis. That's because there is another figure who, in my opinion, is just as influential, yet rarely gets the credit he deserves. His name is Dave Elman (1900-1967), and he wasn't a physician or psychologist. In fact, he had no medical training whatsoever; he was a musician and radio producer. He was also a self-taught expert in hypnosis who began sharing his expertise—primarily with physicians, surgeons, and psychiatrists—in the late 1940s. Some say that Milton Erickson learned much of what he later would be known for from Dave Elman.

GIVING CREDIT TO DOROTHY GATES

Dorothy Gates, Ph.D. was a pioneer in the world of hypnosis. In addition to developing her own company, called Spectra Dynamics, she was an internationally recognized lecturer in the field of self-hypnosis. In addition, Dr. Gates founded The Sunnyside Foundation, a non-profit organization providing research and scholarship in the development of inner resources.

Dorothy has been my guardian angel for most of my life. Most of what I know I learned from her, and the reason I feel so compelled to help others is because she helped me so much, so many times. Thanks to her teachings and guidance, I am who I am today. My only hope for this lifetime is that I have a fraction of the impact on others that Dorothy had on me.

THE BRAIN AND THE MIND: WHERE THE ACTION IS

The brain and the mind have different jobs. In order to understand how hypnosis works, you need to understand what's occurring inside your head as you use self-hypnosis in the process of discovering your inner *self* (your *core*) and reaching your potential.

THE BRAIN

The brain is a physical, tangible thing. It's about three pounds, it has about 30 billion (yes, with a "b") neurons, and it's spongy. You know where it is and roughly what it looks like. It has properties that dictate how it functions, and we know what those properties are. One of them—the one that is most important for hypnosis—is the brainwave.

The level that your brain is operating at dictates how you feel, how you behave, and how you perform. The hypnotic state is attained by taking your brain from Beta, which it's probably in right now, to either the Alpha state or the Theta state, depending on how deeply you need to go for what you'd like to achieve. There's been a lot of research into the four levels of electrical activity that emanate from our brains in the form of brainwaves. Here's a brief review of (or introduction to) the brainwaves and what occurs at each of the four states of consciousness . . .

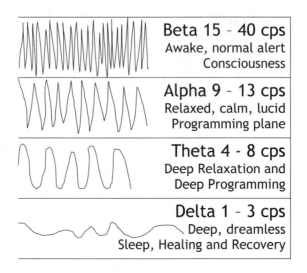

BETA

- The center for logic, analyzing, and reasoning.

- In Beta, you are awake, normal, and alert. This state of consciousness is characterized by sense-experiences: sight, sound, smell, taste, and touch.

- When measuring this state of consciousness on an EEG (electroencephalogram) or other biofeedback machine, we find that it registers at 15-40 cycles per second. (That's fast.)

- At its maximum capacity, Beta comprises only 12% of your total being. Relying on Beta is like relying on a moped to pull a tank.

- The high level of brain activity in Beta significantly affects brain's ability to: store information (memory), access creativity, focus, and concentrate on the workings of the physical body.

- You spend about 90% of the day with your brain in Beta,

but when you get stuck there, tension and negative thinking usually result. The more stressed you feel, the faster your brain will go, and the less likely you are to achieve Alpha, which is where you'd rather be. You'll see glimpses of where you can go and what you can do, but they'll be fleeting.

ALPHA

- Alpha is the strongest, most prominent brain rhythm.
- The optimal state for your brain when you need to be focused and sharp.
- When measuring this state of consciousness on a biofeedback machine, we find that its frequency registers at 9-15 cycles per second.
- The brain's biochemistry is completely balanced in Alpha and the brain functions at optimal level.
- Decision-making at its peak in Alpha.
- This level is necessary in order to achieve behavior modification. In Alpha, you are relaxed, calm, and lucid. This is the programming plane, where you can add new programs and delete old ones. You can also control your dreams while here.
- This is where you are during that first 30 minutes when you are falling asleep, but not quite asleep.

THETA

- This is where you are after that first 30 minutes when you were falling asleep, and before the point when you are sleeping deeply.
- Active dreaming takes place in Theta.
- Theta is level achieved when you're being hypnotized by

someone else, such as during hypnotherapy or stage hypnosis. It's very difficult to reach Theta through self-hypnosis. This is where you can create hallucinations, amnesia, physical perception changes, and deep programming.

- Theta is characterized by deep relaxation and clear mental imagery. This is where you aim to go when you meditate. You can experience painless surgery, dentistry, and childbirth in Theta.
- Brainwave frequency is measured at 5-9 cycles per second.
- In Theta, tasks are so automatic that you aren't consciously aware of what you're doing (like when you drive home and have no recollection of the actual drive).

DELTA

- Deep, dreamless sleep. The body is completely at rest.
- This is where healing and recovery take place.
- The brain operates at 1-5 cycles per second. (That's really, really slow.)

THE MIND

Although the mind isn't something we can point to or describe, there are some things we can say about it. Perhaps the most important conclusion many scientists have reached in the 21st century, is that if all of the organs of the body produce the same chemicals as the brain when it's thinking, the mind comprises the entire body. *The mind's location isn't restricted to the brain; hence, the mind-body connection.*

The easiest way to understand the mind, for the sake of our discussion about hypnosis, is to think of yourself as having basically two minds: your conscious mind and your subconscious mind. Your conscious mind is your thinking, awake state of awareness, yet comprises a remarkably paltry 12% of your mind. Let's see what's in that 12% . . .

Your Conscious Mind

Your conscious mind has *five functions*.
1. Analytical
2. Rational
3. Willpower
4. Working memory
5. Voluntary body functions

HYPNOSIS MODEL

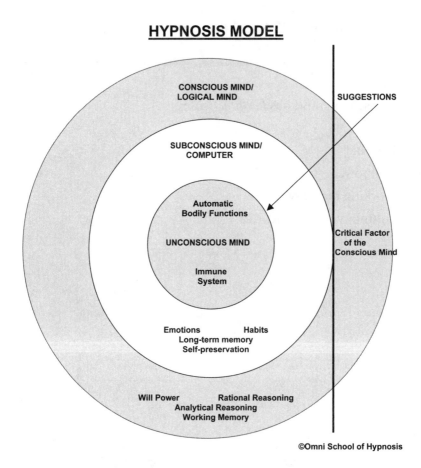

©Omni School of Hypnosis

The Critical Factor works for and protects the subconscious mind but resides in the conscious mind. Hypnosis is the by-pass of the Critical Factor of the conscious mind and the establishment of acceptable selective thinking.

1. ANALYTICAL

Your conscious mind is logical because it is *your analytical mind*. Its job is to analyze problems and figure out how to handle them. This comes in handy when you're trying to figure out how to use the latest new technological gadget.

2. RATIONAL

There's also a *rational part* of your conscious mind. The function of this part of your conscious mind is to give you reasons why you do the things you do. Did you ever notice that you can always come up with logical, sensible reasons for doing the things you do? We call this rationalization. The only problem with this rational reasoning is that even though it's logical, 99% of the time it's incorrect. This is because the true motivation for your behavior and responses comes from a deeper part of the mind that you don't have easy access to when using your conscious mind.

This rational function is important because it allows you to conjure up answers to some very difficult questions. For instance, have you ever asked a smoker why he or she smokes? Your smoker-friend might say something like: "I smoke because it relaxes me and gives me time to pause and gather my thoughts." Even though this isn't the true reason a smoker smokes—and in fact nicotine is a stimulant and doesn't aid in relaxation—it sounds rational and logical and the smoker can comfortably continue to smoke.

Note that the rational function is also the *rational-ization* function, which means it creates lies when you need them (like what your smoker-friend says). The sole job of the conscious mind is to think and provide judgments. And part of its job is to protect the feelings felt by the subconscious mind, which means it will *lie* to protect the subconscious.

Another excellent example of this function is when a client says to me, "I have a great diet plan, but I eat out every night and I eat too late, so I can't stick to it." Meanwhile, the real reason for not sticking to the diet is that the subconscious wants to hold on to the weight because the client feels comfortable with her current habit pattern, which has brought her to her current weight. When she thinks about losing weight, the fear of the unknown (i.e., changing her habit pattern) arises, and she combats that fear by attributing her problem to eating out and eating late. And if that wasn't bad enough, though she continues to say she wants to "lose" weight, like most people, deep down she doesn't like the idea of "loss" or "losing." Her subconscious will help her avoid what she doesn't want: *loss*.

3. WILLPOWER

The next part of the conscious mind is the part you ask to do things it was never meant to do; this is your willpower. Willpower is your ability to control your behavior by stopping and thinking about that behavior first. If you stop and think about what you're going to say or do before you say or do it, you're using your willpower.

Willpower doesn't work very well for changing habits because it's tiring to consciously think before you act for an extended period of time. The moment you let up, the habit comes right back! All of us have tried to change something we think, do, or feel using willpower. Before coming to see me many of my clients tried to use willpower to change bad habits, such as smoking, eating poorly, and not exercising, but they weren't successful. They all had the same result: temporary success, followed by a rebound right back to the habit they were trying to extinguish. And sometimes that habit is even worse on the rebound.

Willpower takes a lot of effort, and you constantly have the feeling of swimming upstream because it assumes that you have something to overcome, and all that does is reinforce that you have something to overcome. You'll see later that when you use your imagination you have the opposite feeling: one of freedom and liberation.

4. WORKING MEMORY

The working memory, or short-term memory, is the only memory you need to get through life on a daily basis. Once a bit of memory no longer serves a useful purpose, it seems to disappear and we seem to forget it (although it doesn't disappear and we don't forget it, in reality). And this is the way it should be. We shouldn't have to remember everything we've experienced, all of the time. That would clutter up our minds too much.

5. VOLUNTARY BODY FUNCTIONS

You can stand when you want to, sit when you want to, and raise your hand when you want to because your conscious mind is able to send messages to what we call your *outer shell*. Your outer shell is composed of the large muscles controlled by the conscious mind. The inner core of your body is the purview of the subconscious mind and includes functions such as: breathing, heart rate, new cell growth, and digestion. This distinction is important because if I asked you to control your digestion, could you do it? I submit that you could, but only by accessing your subconscious through some form of hypnosis.

Notice that all of the above take some kind of effort, or work, in order to succeed at them or do them well. Oddly enough, all that energy that the conscious mind needs accounts for only 12% of your entire mind! If you're thinking that the really important stuff happens elsewhere, you're right. The really important stuff, which takes no conscious energy or effort, takes place in your subconscious mind.

YOUR SUBCONSCIOUS MIND

The subconscious mind is a level of awareness you generally don't have easy access to in a waking state, yet it represents a whopping 88% of your consciousness! Your subconscious has some features that might surprise you . . .

IT'S THE BOSS

Authority means power, right? Well, it probably won't surprise you to discover that there is no power in the conscious mind's measly 12%. That little boss goes through life shouting, talking a mile a minute, thinking, thinking, thinking, and providing color and drive. But it has no power of its own.

The subconscious, on the other hand, is quiet like the night sky or the deep of the ocean. Its single most significant characteristic is that it deals from unawareness. It's completely blind. It doesn't tell you, "Say boss, I picked up some info for you." No, it goes quietly about its business performing all its functions. It's so vast and yet so totally ignored as part of your mentality. In fact, most people go through their entire lives ignoring the fact that it exists. Meanwhile, with only the small 12% working for them, they wonder why life is so difficult. Like an iceberg, the human mind shows only its tip. The rest is hidden out of sight, quiet, dark and ever obedient.

How do we know we have this much power?

Anytime the human body is traumatized, the power within is revealed. We've all heard stories like: A car falls on a teenager while he's underneath it trying to fix it. His 100-pound mother lifts the car several feet off the ground, for several seconds, while her son rolls to safety. Where did she get the power and energy for such a seemingly Herculean feat?

We can allow the mind to function as it was meant to function when we discover how it operates. Reaching the subconscious requires no effort, no concentration. It's simply a matter of allowing, not forcing. As soon as you force (like when you use your willpower), you are sabotaging the ability of your subconscious to give you what you want.

When you allow yourself to relax, you're in the most receptive state of consciousness, and what you want and need flow naturally and freely.

THE SUBCONSCIOUS CAN'T THINK, REASON, OR ARGUE

And it can't judge the merit of an idea, either. But it *can* do something very powerful: It can tell you whether something is smooth or rough, hot or cold, sad or funny, and painful or pleasurable. It feels.

THE SUBCONSCIOUS IS YOUR EMOTIONAL MIND

You have feelings about everything in your life, but most of the time these emotions are beneath your conscious awareness, in your subconscious mind. Ordinarily, when something triggers an emotion, the subconscious opens so you can feel that emotion consciously. As human beings we all get to experience the full range of emotions. That can't be helped and it's usually a blessing.

You learn emotions in different ways: some by direct experience, and others by watching them. Either way, they live in your subconscious, so if you need to change them (like when maybe they are no longer a blessing and they're running your life) you now know where to find them.

YOUR SUBCONSCIOUS = YOU

Who you are, how you respond, and what you believe, are functions of your subconscious mind. All of your automatic responses come from your subconscious mind, including your beliefs. You don't have to stop to figure out what you believe to be true in order to respond to a situation. You simply know what you believe, and your responses are based on your beliefs.

YOUR HABITS ARE A FUNCTION OF YOUR SUBCONSCIOUS MIND

When you do the same thing in the same way, with enough repetition the subconscious mind will make it a habit. A habit is an automatic response, or reminder to respond, to a certain situation in a specific way. Ninety-seven percent of what you do everyday is by habit, and you don't even think about what you're doing. For example, when you get up in the morning and leave the house, at some point you get dressed, right? You don't leave the house and go out in public naked, do you? Have you ever? Why not? Because you have developed a habit pattern, starting when you were a baby, that when you leave the house you must wear clothing. You don't even think about it. In fact, it's such an odd thing to pay attention to, isn't it? That's what happens when you analyze something the subconscious does: it becomes alien to you because you're used to seeing only the result, and not what happens behind the scenes.

Our subconscious has developed habit patterns that help us and haunt us. For instance, we learn that we need to stop at a red light long before we learn how to drive. Being in cars with parents and friends during our childhood and adolescence sends us messages about what you do and don't do when you drive. When the time finally comes when you get behind the wheel and drive off by yourself, you don't give a moment's thought to a red light; you merely slow to a stop. And that habit, whether or not you think of it this way, saves your life.

As for habits that haunt us, I think of people who insist on referring to themselves as "social smokers." They find themselves unconsciously picking up a cigarette when they order a drink or walk into a bar. They've convinced themselves that alcohol and cigarettes "go together," and that "it's natural" to have a drink in one hand and a "butt" in the other. And their subconscious minds must corroborate that idea by creating the behavior to support it. *Luckily, any habit can be changed by working with the subconscious mind through hypnosis (even the habit of calling yourself a social smoker and the habit of smoking).*

EVERYTHING ABOUT YOU IS STORED IN YOUR SUBCONSCIOUS

The subconscious mind stores the memory of not only everything you experience, but also all of your thoughts, fantasies, daydreams, and night dreams. This occurs because *your subconscious mind cannot tell the difference between something that's actually happening to you and something that you're imagining.* The subconscious mind records everything you experience, real and imaginary, as a memory, and reacts to both with the same intensity. Your inner mind cannot tell the difference!

Hypnosis uses that concept to help you reprogram your behavior. Many hypnosis techniques use the imagination to help you actually change what your subconscious is thinking and feeling.

(Note that because of the subjective nature of long-term memory, we never assume that a memory recalled in hypnosis was something that actually happened. We may address it in hypnosis *as if* it really happened, but we would never assume that it had.)

YOUR SUBCONSCIOUS CREATES THE FUTURE

If you fill your subconscious with negative thoughts, feelings and images, you will soon experience the (negative) manifestation of those thoughts feelings and images. Likewise, if you fill your subconscious mind with positive things, you will soon manifest positive things around you. What you think and feel today becomes what you experience in life tomorrow. People who don't realize this, and who experience constant dysfunction, negativity and "bad luck" or "bad karma," don't know that they are basically hypnotizing themselves to attract and create negativity. What you put your energy on is what is created. If your perception is that your life hasn't been full of good things, tell yourself that your past may have been negative, but that time is long gone, and only good things come to you, in abundance.

YOUR SUBCONSCIOUS PROTECTS YOU

An important aspect of your subconscious mind is your protective or self-preserving mind. Its job is to protect you against danger, *both real and imagined*. This is how phobias or irrational fears can develop. The subconscious mind is using a powerful emotion called *fear* to try to protect you from what it believes to be dangerous. For example, if a car veers in front of you, your subconscious will leap to action and tell you to swerve to avoid it. That reflex, in addition to the adrenalin that courses through you and that odd, fluttering feeling that instantly materializes in your stomach, comes from your subconscious.

YOUR SUBCONSCIOUS HOUSES
YOUR IMAGINATION

All of us were born with a marvelous faculty we call imagination. It seems like every child has more than his share. Nevertheless, almost immediately, teachers, parents, and other well-meaning adults attempt to turn it off. We must learn to deal with—and in—"reality," they say. To many people, however, "reality" means worrying, anxiety, hard work, and no fun. And to them, I say, what if everyone in the world turned off his imagination? We would never have anything new. As you may know, Thomas Edison failed 3,000 times when working on the light bulb. He had every reason to give up. In his biography, he talks about how much of the fodder for his continued experimentation arose out of catnaps. The images during his catnaps were the tools his subconscious mind used to explore, communicate and hypothesize.

It's important to know that in the same way the imagination can help you reach your goals, it can *prevent you* from reaching them. Many of the difficulties you experience in your life probably originate in your imagination. And they are so powerful that your mind transforms them into reality. Once again, your 88% overrides your 12%.

Finally, and I'll repeat this later, when you use your imagination, though you must have a clear idea of what you want, you don't want to get bogged down in the minutiae of how'll get it. Your focus is on your destination. *Why?* Because there are many ways to get there. To assume that you know the best way, and to concentrate on that best way, could, in the end, derail you and prevent you from getting what you want. File away your problem-solving skills and your willpower and simply imagine yourself possessing vitality, focus, and good health. Imagine yourself at your best and let your subconscious figure out the most effective way to make your best happen for you.

HOW THE CONSCIOUS AND THE SUBCONSCIOUS WORK TOGETHER

The subconscious and the conscious minds complement each other; they work together, each doing separate tasks. Your subconscious registers your feelings and impressions, and promptly passes them on to the conscious, at which time they register in your awareness.

The only thing the subconscious can do is agree with you; it was designed by nature to be your servant. If you say, "I'm fat and ugly," your subconscious will produce exactly what you tell it to produce. It cannot say No to you.

Think of the mind as operating like a computer. The conscious mind is like the desktop on the display. Imagine the desktop; what's there? The icons for files you're dealing with right now, and the ones you can easily access with the click of a mouse. Meanwhile, your subconscious mind is like hard drive that stores all of your files. Where the heck are they, anyway? Unless you're a computer expert, all you know is that *they're in there somewhere, and they've got all my stuff!* And you also know that without their programs, your information would just be mumbo jumbo.

Regardless of whether you believe your hard drive was empty when you were born or was already filled with thoughts and memories from lives past, it can still be reprogrammed.

Little by little, your hard drive has been programmed by your life experience so that today you are a sum total of everything that has ever happened to you. Everyday, your subconscious mind gets visual input, auditory input, and tactile input totaling 150,000 to 300,000 words and images. Everyday. Everything. Impressions of everything you have ever done, seen, heard, tasted, smelled, or imagined, are all stored somewhere in your subconscious mind. Even images from your peripheral vision—images that you didn't even focus on—have been cataloged and stored in your subconscious.

EVERYTHING?

Yes, because your subconscious holds your long-term memory

(sometimes called permanent memory). Recall that I mentioned that you seem to have forgotten some things from your past. The key word there is *seem*. In reality, you haven't forgotten anything that has happened to you. Every impression is stored somewhere in your subconscious mind. Using certain hypnotherapy techniques, you can recall or re-experience early childhood events, even your birth experiences.

With hypnosis, you can also change your attitudes and beliefs and thereby change your emotional responses. It's possible to reduce guilt, anger, hatred, and resentment, opening you up to experience more emotions such as care, joy and happiness. Who wouldn't want more of those?

You can even strengthen your memory, as deep relaxation brings harmony and close rapport between your conscious and subconscious and makes it easier for them to cooperate. In a state of hypnosis, they work together swimmingly and seamlessly.

How to Observe Your Subconscious in Action

Because this may be your initial exposure to an altered state of consciousness, and in order to give yourself every opportunity to observe your subconscious mind in action, the following exercise will illustrate that:

1. You do have a subconscious mind
2. It does operate effortlessly
3. You can guide and utilize its powers
4. You can tap it for information

Memory exercise

• As you retire for the night, make yourself as comfortable as

possible.
- Close your eyes and relax.
- Ask yourself a question to which you have temporarily forgotten the answer. It can pertain to anything:
  o   the name of an old friend
  o   a long-forgotten teacher
  o   an old address
  o   a phone number
  o   a word in a foreign language that you learned but cannot recall.

Be specific and also be sure that you once knew the information you are requesting. It has to be in there somewhere in order for you to access it. This isn't about creating; it's about *locating*.

- Then, command that sometime during the next day you will have a revelatory thought about your question—that you will suddenly find the answer in your mind and recognize it as the answer.
- Just as soon as you've asked your question and have set the stage for receiving the answer—forget about it and quietly go to sleep. Your subconscious will unfailingly give you the answer to your question if you let it. The same applies for the next day. Stay occupied and don't let your mind wander back on the question. And certainly don't obsess over it. Your subconscious cannot function as directed if your conscious mind is constantly interfering.
- When you least expect it, the answer will appear.

Let's review the properties of the conscious mind and the subconscious mind . . .

Conscious Mind/Monitor	Subconscious Mind/Hard Drive
12%	88%
Master	Servant
Effect	Cause
Thinking	Feeling
Perception	Blindness
Awareness	Involuntary
Will	Power
Activity	Quiet
Light	Darkness
Objective	Subjective

Hypnosis is simply about making a change in the subconscious mind. This is very powerful because if a suggestion is allowed to go into your subconscious mind, then it has the power to change your beliefs and change your behaviors. So how does a suggestion get into your subconscious? In other words, how does hypnosis happen?

THE CRITICAL FACTOR OF THE CONSCIOUS MIND

There's another part of the mind, which operates automatically when you're using your conscious mind. Dave Elman called it the **critical factor** of the conscious mind, and it acts as a critic or a judge of all suggestions presented to you. Its job is to protect the status quo of your beliefs in your subconscious mind. This is an important function because if you didn't have it, anyone could walk up to you and say something to manipulate you. When you hear a suggestion, your critical factor checks with your subconscious mind to see if that suggestion is in agreement with your existing beliefs. If it is, the suggestion is allowed to go into your subconscious and the belief is made stronger. If it isn't, the suggestion is rejected and there is no change.

You can see the critical factor in action when you try to discuss religion or politics with someone who has different beliefs than you. Because the critical factor doesn't allow the opposing belief to enter the subconscious, you keep steadfast to your own thoughts. So how do we get suggestions into that subconscious mind? How can we effect change of belief and habits? We use hypnosis.

Hypnosis bypasses the critical factor of the conscious mind in order to open the door to your subconscious mind (i.e., your hard drive) and focus the mind to accept positive information, such as encouraging suggestions. In other words, a hypnotist is a kind of human computer re-programmer. If an idea is permitted to enter into your subconscious, you are positioned to change. In fact, you will automatically begin to respond differently.

In hypnosis, we push the conscious mind aside. Adults have a very hardcore critical faculty made up of all of the facts and figures and nonsense they have picked up through the years. This critical faculty will leap to the defense of any preconditioned idea and instantly refute it. So let's say an overweight woman is lying on the couch—not in Alpha—just lying there. Let's say I tell this individual: "You are slender." She will get up and say, "Are you out of your mind? I look in the mirror and I can see what I am. I'm fat!" Do you hear what she is putting into her subconscious mind?

In Alpha and Theta, however, there's just no way the woman can fight the idea of being thin. She'll just drift off while the "You are Slender"—idea goes right into her subconscious mind. It will bypass her critical factor and grow stronger and stronger as it is reapplied over and over. Eventually, the notion of thin is stronger than the notion of fat and *presto*, she manifests thin physically because her subconscious mind says that's what's real.

WHY A HYPNOTIST CAN'T CONTROL YOU . . .

Now if this was all there was to hypnosis, we hypnotists would be able to control our clients. All hypnotists would be millionaires, and we'd all be thin, for sure. But since we know that's not the case, I want to address the one element to hypnosis that prevents a hypnotist from being able to control you: You never lose the awareness of the suggestions given to you.

Yes, when you enter hypnosis the critical factor is bypassed, but now your conscious mind takes on the important job of protecting you against suggestions that aren't good for you or that you don't whole-heartedly want. You see, when you're in hypnosis, you can hear perfectly everything that's going on. Actually, all of your five senses become sharper and more powerful. Your state of awareness is heightened and your ability to decide what you will and won't do, or what you will or won't accept, is much stronger when you're in hypnosis. So you see, your conscious mind is still aware and you can hear every suggestion that is given to you.

YOU'VE BEEN HYPNOTIZED
THOUSANDS OF TIMES

A hypnotic state (also called a trance) is a natural state of mind. Believe it or not, you go in and out of hypnotic trances all day long. You'd be surprised just how many times your critical factor is being bypassed everyday. For example, we've all heard of highway hypnosis. That's when you're driving down the road and you don't remember driving the last block or maybe the last several miles or perhaps you missed your turn. That's because while you were daydreaming, your subconscious mind took over driving for your own protection.

We tend to zone out and get very relaxed while watching television, one of the great hypnotizers. Sometimes we even ignore things going on around us when watching television. Add to that the fact that advertisers know everything hypnotists know about bypassing your critical factor. Advertisers use that knowledge to suggest to you or to hypnotize you into buying their products. Branding experts, in particular, use the principles of hypnosis to persuade you that you simply must acquire *the feeling* that the brand will give you: that you must buy their products because you can't be happy or whole without them. Think of how mindlessly you walk through a department store, directly to the brand—the designer—whose clothes you ordinarily buy. Why?

Authority figures can also bypass your critical factors. For example, you'll tend to believe people you look up to: those whom you think know more than you do. This includes doctors, schoolteachers, preachers, and motivational speakers. All kinds of people bypass your critical factor. Anytime you're feeling a strong emotion such as love or fear, anger or grief, you are more suggestible. Things said to you, or things you say to yourself, will bypass your critical factor and become part of your subconscious programming. So you see, you don't have to be in any kind of relaxed state at all to accept suggestion. You don't even need to close your eyes. We call this waking hypnosis, and it happens everyday.

Using Hypnosis to Extinguish Fears and Phobias

Phobias, extreme anxiety, some fears, and excessive behaviors can all be extinguished through hypnosis, although they require more than just the average positive suggestion to impact them significantly. We don't develop phobias out of a habit, but rather because of some situation that profoundly frightened us in the past. Usually, this situation occurred during early childhood, yet we continue to relive it—and even exaggerate it. For example, most people have fear of public speaking to some degree and many people are terrified of snakes, spiders, flying, or heights. We learn these fears from early experiences, sometimes long forgotten. With hypnotherapy techniques, you can remove your fear by changing the response where it lives in the subconscious mind.

But you have to have the right attitude . . .

ATTITUDE IS EVERYTHING

The mental attitude you hold when you hear a suggestion determines whether it goes into your internal computer in order for change to begin, or whether it's rejected and there will be no change.

Three Attitudes Affect Your Hypnotic State

1.   The first mental attitude you can hold when you hear a
     suggestion is: "Boy I like that suggestion. I know that it's
     going to work beautifully for me!" Yes, and it will. This
     attitude means that you passionately want and trust the
     suggestion, and it should be allowed into your subconscious
     mind. And because the suggestion is allowed to go into your
     subconscious computer, the change happens.

The other two mental attitudes will cause you to reject the suggestion, and there will be no change at all. They are:

2. If you're thinking: "I don't know, there's just something a little uncomfortable about that suggestion," you'll reject suggestions for change of things you feel strongly about, such as your morals or religion. In short, there won't be any change.

3. Finally, you can also be neutral. For example, you don't care if you get it or you don't get it, but you're willing to try new things. Unfortunately, there's not enough energy behind that suggestion for it to make much of an impression, so it's rejected and there's no change. If you've ever heard someone say something like, "I tried hypnosis and it didn't work," that's because, providing they went into hypnosis in the first place, they've probably held on to this last mental attitude and caused their own failure. When they heard a suggestion they said to themselves, "I like that suggestion. I sure hope it works." What they didn't realize was that hope means doubt, and doubt rejects the suggestion. (There's much more about words and how your subconscious interprets them later.)

If you hope it's going to work, you really don't believe it's going to work, and that instructs your mind to reject the suggestion. You can hope all day long that I'm going to make you change, and it simply won't happen. I cannot control you. But if you want the change and you focus on the suggestion with a positive attitude, trusting that it will work, the suggestion will be allowed in and positive change will definitely happen!

Don't be neutral. Embrace the mental attitude that says, "I really like that suggestion, and I know it's going to work for me." When you do that, hypnosis can make changes happen so easily it seems like magic. So you see, you're the one who's in control; you determine whether or not you can change with hypnosis. When you allow your hypnotist to bypass your critical factor and introduce the suggestions you want, you will get the change you desire.

YOUR *DISCOVER PROCESS*
SELF-HYPNOSIS SESSIONS

In the field of hypnosis, we use the word *session* to describe the physical act of reaching the subconscious mind, either through listening to a CD or reading a self-hypnosis script. This natural technique is so effective at releasing all muscle and nerve tension within the body that you immediately experience a wonderful sense of well-being and ease. This deep state of rest is accompanied by an improvement in circulation. And your mind, free from tension and useless activity, is able to strengthen and re-energize every muscle, every nerve, and every cell in your body. By releasing deep muscular tension (perhaps for the first time in your life), you alleviate nerve tension automatically. And with freedom from nerve tension comes absolute and complete relaxation.

Relaxation is achieved during the session by means of suggestion. As you relax your mind by letting it dwell upon thoughts of quietness, serenity, and well-being, your body quickly responds to the suggestion of rest by letting go and relaxing. To realize a progressively deeper state of relaxation, all you need to do is maintain this calm, quiet state of mind.

The vital point to remember while attaining the state of deep relaxation is:

Make absolutely no effort to achieve it. No concentration or effort is necessary. Simply let it happen.

Effort is the function of the conscious mind. The subconscious mind does everything with ease. It is the subconscious you are working with during your sessions. Since it learns very quickly, your subconscious will soon anticipate what it must do so that with each repetition of the relaxation routine, you relax easier, faster, and deeper.

RULES FOR SUCCESSFUL SELF-HYPNOSIS SESSIONS

You will first learn a few basic rules, and then you must practice, practice, practice. Repetition is your friend. As we say in yoga: repetition is the mother of mastery.

RULE #1: PRESET YOUR TIME LIMIT.

- Twenty minutes is the optimal amount of time, but you can use five or ten minutes if that's all you have.
- Give your subconscious the command that under no circumstances will you exceed the time limit. Remember, your subconscious must obey you. If you find yourself exceeding your time period (especially in the beginning), it may signify that you are releasing a great amount of tension. Only in the beginning and only under extreme stress should you lengthen the time period of practice. If you must, use a timer or alarm to awaken you until you have trained the subconscious to respond to you. Some of you awaken in the morning without a clock. This works in the same way. Your eyes will pop open, you will have a twitch or your leg will jump. Something will awaken you. You are seeking a dreamy, detached state (not sleep) wherein you can make clear and definite impressions upon your feeling mind. Total

unawareness does not mean sleep. It is merely an indication that you are at a very deep level of Alpha.

Rule #2: Get comfortable.

- Loosen your clothing if it is at all tight or binding. Remove your shoes, your tie, or any article of clothing that may pinch you or be uncomfortable in any way. Position yourself so that your circulation is not restricted. Arms at sides, palms up, legs uncrossed, glasses removed. If you sleep with your contacts, leave them in; if not, remove them.

Rule #3: Initially use the same place to practice.

- You will begin to associate the chair, couch, bed, or even floor with the Alpha level of consciousness. As you become accustomed to the routine, habit takes over and you will find yourself propelled to that place at approximately the same hour each day. Think of this relaxation period as you would a daily bath—except this bath is for your mind. If you might be doing your self-hypnosis at work, as well, choose a spot there and form the habit of going to that spot for practice.
- Don't use your bed if you have difficulty sleeping. Don't use your ex-husband's or ex-wife's chair (there are negative connotations attached). Don't practice for at least an hour before bedtime—otherwise you will be alert and awake when you want to sleep.

Rule #4: Use your environment.

- Allow every noise, sound, or movement to carry you deeper into the desired state. We live in a noise-filled, busy, active world. To be completely effective you must be able to achieve this state of Alpha any time you choose, under any conditions. To do this, simply use your immediate environment to help you relax instead of working to discount it. Prepare for eventuality. If you are expecting a call, use a telephone to awaken you. If the doorbell should ring, use it to deepen the state. It is up to you to form the habit. Every sound or noise can take you deeper and deeper or it can awaken you. It's your choice.

RULE #5: ALWAYS MAINTAIN THE SAME ATTITUDE.

- "Here I go!" Expect to thoroughly enjoy this period of relaxation. Assume an attitude of: "I allow myself to relax as deeply as I can and I enjoy the benefit from the experience." Avoid analyzing, avoid questioning and give up trying. Simply let it happen.

AUTOMATIC RESULTS FROM PRACTICING

The results of practicing include: you sleep better, your mental and physical health improve, and your performance at work improves. Without the continual carryover of tension from day to day, your systems function more efficiently. You are more at ease during both your waking and sleeping hours, and you sleep deeper and more contently, but for a shorter period of time. Twenty minutes in Alpha is equal to four hours of natural rest. When you find yourself sleeping less, you will also find yourself with extra hours to do those things you have always wanted to do—extra reading, writing, exercising, whatever interests you.

CONDITIONING YOURSELF
TO REACH ALPHA STATE

Once you are able to consciously relax your mind and your body, you will be prepared to go into Alpha state using the "Alpha Conditioning" script that follows this section. And once in Alpha, you will be ready to put yourself into a hypnotic state and accept the suggestions that will lead to changes in your behavior on a deep, subconscious level.

You are probably going to have to practice a handful of times, with the complete or extended script in order to achieve the Alpha state necessary for you to accept the direct suggestions in the hypnosis script or CD. You can either read the following script, record yourself reading it (and be prepared to do it a couple of times until you get it right), or you can listen to the progressive relaxation ("Alpha Conditioning") segment, which is at the beginning of every CD in the Perfect Enough CD package.

For each Key, beginning with Self Confidence (which also contains the Release & Clear Script), you'll chart your progress over 21 days, by placing checkmarks in the following grid:

S	M	T	W	Th	F	Sat

You'll mark each successive time you read or listen to a script. If you skip a day, you must start over. After you have had 21 successive sessions for a script, you may move on to the next one. Please use the Self Hypnosis Instruction Chart at the end of this chapter to help you stay on track.

Let's relax using Alpha Conditioning. Read the following script . . .

EXTENDED ALPHA CONDITIONING SCRIPT

Under no circumstances do I naturally fall asleep. I allow myself to relax . . . I relax and allow myself to become as comfortable as possible. I feel myself relax. I allow the sensation of gentle rest to begin flowing throughout my body. I can feel myself growing more and more relaxed with each and every breath that I exhale. I visualize a balloon exhausting all its air. I too relax, releasing greater and greater amounts of tension as I exhale . . . dissolving into the deepest state of rest. I feel . . . feel . . . the sensation of soothing relaxation as it begins in my toes . . . and each and every fiber and muscle in each toe now responds to the irresistible urge to let go . . . to let go. Each toe grows limp, loose, and relaxed. As a dry sponge absorbs warm, languid liquid . . . my body absorbs the soothing, languid, glowing quietness . . . of relaxation. Irresistibly . . . the relaxation flows into both of my feet. Smoothly yet quickly, with an ever-increasing sense of pleasure and enjoyment, the sense of peaceful, calm relaxation reaches my knees . . . and my knees relax. Swiftly now, like that thirsty sponge . . . soaking up warm liquid, the relaxation spreads to my upper legs, saturating them . . . spreading smoothly into both hips, and I am, from the hips all the way down to the tips of my toes . . . firmly aware . . . and yet deeply relaxed.

With every breath now, my level of conscious awareness grows less and less . . . and less. Feeling safe and secure, my legs seem to fade . . . fade . . . fade away. Every breath is slow and easy . . . slow and easy . . . slow and easy. As I relax deeper and deeper, the same soothing, tingling . . . relaxation . . . now begins to develop in my fingertips, filling each finger smoothly, deeply, and totally, with the sensation of deep relaxation. Each finger discharges every last bit of muscular tension, and in doing so . . . grows limp, loose, and relaxed. As the relaxation grows deep and complete, it spills over into both of my hands, saturating every tissue . . . every fiber . . . every cell . . . with the most enjoyable sensation . . . of absolute ease and quietness. As tension is dissipated, I become aware of the sensation of the free-flowing circulation of my blood, which adds to the glow of relaxation. Both my hands are now completely relaxed . . . and the relaxation spreads with increasing effectiveness into my wrists, and my wrists let go . . . into my forearms . . . and they, too, grow limp and relaxed. My elbows let go as they too . . . seem to fade . . . fade . . . fade away.

Swiftly now, the growing sensation of utter calmness and tranquility permeates my upper arms . . . the muscles grow limp and relaxed . . . and finally permeates both shoulders and . . . my shoulders let go . . . very limp, very relaxed. With each soothing, satisfying breath, they seem to fade . . . fade . . . fade . . . from my conscious awareness. My legs are deeply relaxed, and my arms are deeply relaxed. A soothing, penetrating . . . deep quietness of my arms and legs now begins to penetrate, to saturate . . . to fill and to soak . . . the rest of my body . . . with calm, quiet rest. I visualize clear, golden honey flowing smoothly and gently into a clear, glass container. Like the honey, the relaxation spills down from my shoulders, flows down my spinal column . . . bubbling up from my hips . . . and through my body . . . slowly filling me with the most pleasant, enjoyable sensation of quietness. My back muscles relax . . . my abdomen muscles relax . . . my chest muscles relax . . . and every tissue, every organ, every gland, deep within my being responds to this soothing sensation . . . by relaxing also. Relax . . . relax . . . relax.

Every sound, every noise, every voice that I hear helps me to relax deeper and deeper. My glands and my organs are smoothly and efficiently . . . growing even more relaxed with each and every beat of my heart. My heart is now pumping soothing . . . easy . . . quietness throughout my being. Slowly and irresistibly now, my entire body is filling . . . filling . . . filling . . . with relaxation . . . and soon, my entire body grows limp and then begins to fade . . . fade . . . fade away. As my conscious mind yields to its critical authority . . . as it drifts . . . and dreams . . . and floats . . . the irresistible sensation of relaxation spreads smoothly into the muscles of my neck and each nerve, each muscle, each fiber . . . grows limp and relaxes, responding more and more to the urge to relax . . . deeper and deeper. As my neck muscles relax, all congestion is relieved, all tension vanishes . . . and the sensation of utter contentment fills my mind. My mind urges my relaxed body to let go even more. The soothing quietness spreads into my scalp . . . and my entire scalp lets go.

A blanket of quietness is slowly enveloping my entire being, which I can now feel. I feel a cap of soothing, drowsy rest spreading over my entire scalp, and with such ease . . . with such enormous pleasure . . . the languid warmth finally spreads down across my face and every muscle . . . every nerve . . . every fiber in my face grows limp and relaxed. The muscles in my cheeks and jaws let go. I am now completely and totally relaxed. Every breath takes me deeper and deeper. Every breath finds me with less and less conscious awareness, but with greater and greater receptivity of my subconscious mind. I am, from this time forward, growing more relaxed, serene, and calm during all my waking and sleeping hours. I can, at any time, achieve this same deep sense of relaxation and quietness. I have the ability to relax and I do so with the greatest ease and pleasure . . . making relaxation the easiest thing I do.

Upon awakening . . . I find I am more refreshed and more invigorated than I have ever felt in my whole life. I always find relaxation refreshing . . . invigorating . . . rejuvenating.

You now have the choice to either awaken or to drift off into a normal, natural sleep. If you are going to awaken, say:

Twenty minutes. Wide awake.

If you are going to drift off into a normal, natural sleep, say:

I am now going to drift off into a normal, natural sleep. When I awaken, I will feel fully rested, calm, and at peace with myself, the world, and those around me.

Once you have completed the above program, you can progress to a more immediate form of Alpha conditioning . . .

INSTRUCTIONS FOR INSTANT ALPHA CONDITIONING

Assuming you practiced the extended Alpha script, several times, under the proper conditions, you should easily be able to progress from the extended script to accessing Alpha state by using a single word (you meditators out there will already be familiar with this process, and whatever mantra you currently use will work just fine for our purposes here).

1. Select a word you would like to use to replace the Alpha conditioning technique introduced above.
2. Practice this for one week. If Alpha state occurs when you use the chosen word, go on with the program. If not, repeat this set of instructions until Alpha occurs using your chosen word. When Alpha consistently occurs, you can use this technique to prepare your mind prior to any of the self-hypnosis scripts.

INSTANT ALPHA CONDITIONING SCRIPT

From this moment on, each and every time I desire to attain the deep state of total relaxation, I am instantly and fully relaxed, as I am now drifting into the Alpha state of consciousness. The moment I think my chosen word, _____, Alpha occurs. This word has an effect only when I use it and only under the proper circumstances. Each and every time I do use it I am fully prepared to receive positive, beneficial and constructive suggestions, impressing each one deeper into my storage and memory facility of my brain.

From this moment on, _____ triggers deep relaxation of my mind and body. I feel Alpha occur. I feel wonderful. I feel comfortable. I am totally receptive and responsive to my own creative ideas and suggestions. I am bathed in a glow of quietness, peace, and serenity. My chosen word works only when I deliberately use it for deep relaxation to attain Alpha consciousness. Its use in regular conversation has no effect on me whatsoever. From this moment on, each and every time I desire the deep state of total relaxation, I am instantly and fully relaxed upon saying _____. Because my subconscious must follow my command, each and every time I desire total relaxation, I am instantly and fully relaxed when I think my chosen word_____ _____. I feel a deep sense of gratification as this word programming becomes a reality. Feeling wonderful, generous, alive, and eager to awaken . . .

You now have the choice to either awaken or to drift off into a normal, natural sleep. If you are going to awaken, say:

Twenty minutes. Wide awake.

If you are going to drift off into a normal, natural sleep, say:

I am now going to drift off into a normal, natural sleep. When I awaken, I will feel fully rested, calm, and at peace with myself, the world, and those around me.

THE POWER OF COMPOUNDING

You'll be using your ability to access Alpha throughout Perfect Enough. In each of the Keys to the **DISCOVER PROCESS**, you'll have opportunities to use your subconscious to create balance and happiness in your life. At the end of each script for the Keys, you'll notice a sentence that looks something like this:

This entire suggestion is represented by the letter "D" of my sub-key word "Discover." Anytime I think, say, or see the word "Discover," all suggestions keyed to this word are automatically activated, stimulated and work for my benefit.

Each of the eight sessions is associated with a letter in **DISCOVER**. This technique is called compounding, the effect of which is that each time you see, hear, or say the word **DISCOVER**, all of the effects of your sessions are triggered and made exponentially more powerful. You need to remember the word **DISCOVER** at least once every 36 hours to get the full effect. Here are the eight Keys to the **DISCOVER PROCESS**:

D   21 sessions of Self-Confidence

I   21 sessions of Self-Talk

S   21 sessions of Persistence

C   21 sessions of Life & Aliveness

O   21 sessions of Health

V   21 sessions of Love

E   21 sessions of Prosperity

R   21 sessions of Meaning

Before we move on to the Keys, we first must discuss the other two tools that you'll be using to achieve balance and happiness: Neuro-Linguistic Programming (NLP), and the Natural Laws of the Mind and the Laws of the Universe.

CHAPTER 2

WHAT IS NEURO-LINGUISTIC PROGRAMMING, AND WHY DO YOU NEED IT?

NEURO-LINGUISTIC PROGRAMMING (NLP) IS used by millions of people around the world in a variety of fields, including: sports, business, education, therapy, and personal development (think Anthony Robbins). Though there isn't one definitive version of the history of NLP that all of the parties involved agree on, everyone does agree that two twenty-somethings at the University of California at Santa Cruz started NLP in the early 1970s. Richard Bandler, a psychology student, and John Grinder, an associate professor of linguistics, began studying the thinking and behavioral skills used by particularly effective and successful people.

Two of the successful people Bandler and Grinder studied were Virginia Satir (who's considered the mother of Family Therapy) and Fritz Perls (the founder of Gestalt Therapy). They were able to extract the thoughts and behaviors that they felt were largely responsible for the success of Satir, Perls, and the others they studied, and they presented their findings in workshops.

Bandler and Grinder were introduced to the work of Milton

Erickson, and began pondering hypnotic techniques in addition to their growing (and by then diverse) body of knowledge about effectiveness and success that they called NLP. Their initial target audience were therapists, and they published books, facilitated seminars and workshops, and produced a cadre of students, some of whom went on to start their own NLP centers.

By the early 1980s, Bandler and Grinder went their separate ways. But NLP kept growing and diversifying, with an increasingly strong presence in England. It was officially becoming a movement.

WHAT EXACTLY IS NLP?

NLP has been called an owner's manual for your brain. It has also been called the study of excellence, the study of success, and the science of achievement. And all that is accurate. NLP is a practical explanation of how to succeed. It's based on observable phenomena, not theories, and it works. Most important, it's a simple process:

1. NLP examines success for its underlying patterns of thought, belief, and behavior.
2. It seeks to reproduce the thoughts, beliefs, and behaviors that create success, thereby reproducing success.

And when I refer to success, I mean in communication, in relationships, and in work. Success in being YOU. The name Neuro-Linguistic Programming describes this system for success perfectly:

N = Neuro, referring to the mind (and particularly its connection to the body)
L = Linguistic, referring to the potential for change using language

P = Programming, meaning the study of patterns that create
  success and failure, and programming yourself with the
  success-patterns

Therefore, if you would like to improve your self-image in a short
period of time, NLP can help you. It has been helping millions of
people for three decades, and it's probably the easiest thing you can
do to improve your life.

When you become knowledgeable and, more important, skilled,
in the techniques of NLP, you'll be able to:

- Learn new things faster than before.
- Master what you can already do well.
- Manage your emotions more effectively.
- Improve your relationships.
- Communicate more effectively.
- Think more clearly.
- Create healthier, more positive behaviors.
- Concentrate better.
- Have the courage to become who you want to be.
- Enjoy life more than ever before.

LET'S GET STARTED!

If you want to produce any kind of lasting change in your behavior,
the decision to change is your first step. Then comes learning whatever
it is you need to learn to create your change. The final part, which is
probably most important, is practice.

I constantly hear people saying things like, "I'm going to take
control of my finances this year" or "This is the year I'm going to lose
weight and start exercising."

What keeps many people from accomplishing these types of goals is simple: we get attached to our past. For example, I have a client who has been married three times and is terrified of making another commitment. She simply looks at her track record—which says to her that she has already failed three times—and she is convinced that she will never be able to succeed. But all she has to do is learn what a good relationship looks like and feels like, then create that behavior from the outside in.

The bottom line is that we ought to learn from past mistakes and make adjustments in future behavior. The strategy of berating yourself for past conduct solves nothing and only serves to lower your self-esteem. You create a vicious cycle where negative experiences and negative feelings are reinforced, which leads to more negative outcomes and more negative feelings.

To create a different result, you must create new, more positive behaviors to replace the old ones that got you the old results. As they say, the definition of insanity is *doing the same thing over and over and expecting a different result.*

Neuro-Linguistic Programming is a great way to be the you you were meant to be, but if you want to accelerate your progress, you need to use NLP in conjunction with hypnosis. Hypnosis and NLP are like eating well and exercising: you'll lose weight if you do them separately, but when you do them together, you'll lose more weight, faster. You'll turbo-charge your weight loss.

NLP ESSENTIALS

NLP techniques set out to alter our verbal and nonverbal communication so we produce the results and reactions we intend to produce. There are plenty of books on NLP in your local library and your local bookstore, and there are several websites dedicated to it. And while there are some subtle and not-so-subtle differences in interpretations of NLP and its use, there are also some essentials that everyone agrees on. Here's a set of essential principles of NLP, which we call *presuppositions*. No matter who you are, how much money you have, how much you weigh, or how long you've been unhappy, these will be true for you.

- **There is no such thing as failure. There is only feedback.**

If you are regularly successful at anything, chances are you have developed patterns of thoughts, feelings, and actions that have left little room for any other outcome. With a few exceptions, there are no flukes when it comes to outcome. Every outcome, whether you view it as a failure or a success, is really just an outcome. And every outcome has a clear path that leads to it.

We're all products of patterns that we have created—consciously and unconsciously—for our entire lives. Nothing about us is because of chance. This can be good, as we may have developed patterns that serve us: that work for us. But it can also be bad, as we have unwittingly developed patterns that are destructive, or at best unproductive.

Therefore, according to NLP there is no such thing as failure; there is only feedback. And if the feedback you have isn't what you wanted, you should change what you did in order to change the feedback. If you want new results, change yourself. After all, it's easier than trying to change anyone else.

How do you change yourself?

By creating a list of behaviors that work and don't work in your life. If you work backwards from your successes and your failures, you can list what you did that caused the outcome. That's NLP: a set of descriptions about what works and what doesn't. There's no judgment about good and bad; there's simply what works and what doesn't work.

- **THE MEANING OF A COMMUNICATION IS THE RESPONSE YOU GET.**

Though you have an intention behind your communication, that intention is meaningless unless it matches the message that those around you receive. You can usually tell what message has been received, as people will respond in a way that tells you. If you haven't been as successful as you would like in getting the outcomes you desire, chances are you have developed patterns of thoughts and feelings that have left little room for any other outcome. You may not be getting the response you want, but you'll always get a response to what the other person heard.

- **THE MAP IS NOT THE TERRITORY.**

NLP is about altering your perceptions, as they are what define what you call "reality." Let's think of your perception about, say, your inability to make a lot of money because you haven't in the past, as your "map" of reality regarding your ability to generate income. Though your map was true for the past, it isn't necessarily true for the present "territory" you are in. You have programmed yourself to use a certain map, and though it doesn't relate to your current conditions, your brain will continue to use it again and again, unless and until you tell it not to and you present it with a more powerful map. There's a high probability that the maps you are using regarding your worthiness and self-image don't correspond to the territory you are navigating, yet you use them anyway, and they steer you back to the old destination.

The **DISCOVER PROCESS** is a way to create new maps (and/ or improve the ones you already have) for how you navigate areas regarding self-confidence, love, health, and prosperity. With those new maps, you'll be equipped to improve the quality of your life and achieve your goals faster and more efficiently, and all while increasing your happiness.

• YOU ARE NOT BROKEN. WHATEVER IT IS YOU ARE ACCOMPLISHING, YOU HAVE WORKED FLAWLESSLY TO GET TO THIS POINT.

Each of us is exactly where we are meant to be in order to get closer to our destiny at every moment. There is nothing "wrong" with any of us; we are all Perfect Enough. For instance, I have a client who has a fear of flying. She views that fear as negative and as evidence that she is "broken." But her fear of flying works perfectly every time. She never makes a reservation without feeling her fear. Now, I'm not saying her fear is useful for her, but it is part of a system she has developed that is flawless. If she doesn't change something about the system and interrupt the way it functions, she'll keep getting the same, predictable result.

• IF YOU ALWAYS DO WHAT YOU'VE ALWAYS DONE, YOU'LL ALWAYS GET WHAT YOU'VE ALWAYS GOT.

This presupposition echoes the previous one in that if you don't change a variable in an equation, you'll continually get a certain result. Two plus three will always equal five unless you change one of the numbers, the plus sign, or the signs of the numbers (i.e., make them negative instead of positive). Similarly, if you don't change something about the way you approach flying when you ordinarily have a fear of it, then you'll continue to experience the fear.

• YOU ALREADY HAVE ALL OF THE RESOURCES YOU NEED.

This is the "ruby slipper" presupposition. Dorothy always had the ability to get back to Kansas, but she didn't know it. She didn't know how to use her ruby slippers. Likewise, if you don't know how to use your brain, and you aren't aware of your innate ability to change your life by changing your mind, then you will always be in search of the Wizard of Oz.

• YOU CANNOT **NOT** COMMUNICATE.

Think about it. Everything someone else can see, hear, or feel, that is coming from you, is communicating something about what you are thinking and feeling. From body language to eye movement, to tone of voice, to the speed of your breath and the pace of your speech. We all communicate virtually all the time—we can't help it.

Some of the things that come from you that affect others are in your control, and others don't appear to be. Emotions, for instance, begin internally. Then they produce physiological changes that occur in the human body that tend to produce predictable outer manifestations of those emotions. Here are a few examples of this phenomenon.

ANGER

When you're angry your heart and breathing rates jump, your blood flows to your hands in preparation to hit something, and your overall energy increases. The volume and projection of your voice also increase, in order to attempt to instill fear in anyone who is threatening to you.

FEAR

When you're in fear, your heart and breathing speed up, but your blood takes a different direction; it leaves your face and surges to your legs for a quick escape (the flight portion of Fight or Flight—see above for the fight part). Momentarily, your body freezes, making it possible to determine if hiding would be better than running. The volume and projection of your voice lessen to minimize the potential of drawing attention.

DISGUST

Disgust is usually indicated by the shunning of your senses. For instance, your eyes squint, your face turns away, your lips curl, and your nose wrinkles. Your vocalization becomes staccato and is marked by quick, short outbursts of breath, similar to what you do when you spit out unwanted food.

LOVE

Love is a relaxed state marked by increasing blood flow to the lips and hands accompanied by an open physical bearing and deep breathing, which facilitate contentment and cooperation. Vocalization becomes more resonant, perhaps to soothe and charm.

- **WHAT YOU THINK IS WHAT YOU GET.**

I've found that there are four mental-conditioning laws for the conscious mind that are particularly helpful to my clients:

1. You are what you concentrate on.
2. What you concentrate on seems real (because real and imagined cannot be discerned).
3. What you concentrate on grows.
4. You always find what you concentrate on.

- # YOU DON'T KNOW WHAT YOU DON'T KNOW.

In NLP's model of learning, we call this unconscious incompetence. Experts/coaches/ therapists/ hypnotherapists are helpful because you don't know what you don't know. But once you do, you are at the point of choice. Then, you know what you don't know, and you can choose to do something about it.

In NLP, when we achieve excellence, we say that we have evolved from . . .

unconscious incompetence → conscious incompetence →
conscious competence → unconscious competence

After some training and practicing, you become aware of what you're doing to be successful; you've reached the state of conscious competence. And finally, you reach a state where you are no longer aware of thinking about what you are doing to achieve success. This is your ultimate goal, and it is called unconscious competence.

- # IF ONE PERSON CAN DO SOMETHING, YOU CAN LEARN IT, TOO.

This doesn't mean that you can sing like Celine Dion just because you both have vocal cords. But it does mean that you can learn from her success. She sang as a child, developed certain habits regarding improving her singing and developing a career, and then as an adult, she nurtured her talent and her career in a certain way. There is always something we can learn from the success of others. We might not be physically able to duplicate what they do, but that doesn't mean we can't improve what we're doing.

The fastest way toward excellence is to find someone who already exhibits it and do what they do. NLP uses several techniques to produce and reproduce excellence. The ones I use most in my practice are:

- Modeling
- Circle of Excellence
- Theater of the Mind
- Anchoring

Modeling

The theory of **Modeling** says that we can achieve excellence in anything by finding a place where it already exists and copying the traits and behaviors present when excellence is present. Everyone needs a role model, and this takes the use of the role model a step farther in that you'll actually *model the behavior of the role model.*

- Imagine someone living life with ease, poise, confidence . . . balanced. Keep that image in your mind for a moment.
- Look at the person's body, their smile, their posture, their eyes. Memorize the person. Put yourself in their position. Imagine yourself looking that happy, fit, and balanced.
- What are you thinking about that allows you to be in that position? What are you feeling?

These are the thoughts and feelings you want to develop. This is modeling.

Meanwhile, back in your real life . . .

When you are getting ready for your day in the morning, what do you ordinarily think about? What do you feel? What ordinarily occurs?

- Are you thinking about work?
- Are you thinking about the last conversation you had with your spouse?
- Are you thinking about how you are going to lose weight?
- Are you thinking about your financial situation?

When you think about all of the negative aspects of your life, you create negative thoughts inside you, and you shouldn't be surprised when your day doesn't measure up. What you think is what you get.

CIRCLE OF EXCELLENCE

The **Circle of Excellence** is the people and images, sights and sounds, you surround yourself with that are indicative of excellence, and that exude excellence.

Imagine yourself in the middle of a circle, and then fill that circle with whatever has contributed to your excellence and whatever is proof of your excellence. Accessing that mental image—and its corresponding confidence, self-esteem, life and aliveness—recreates that excellence. Remember, the subconscious mind responds as if that circle is your reality.

Note that when NLP refers to excellence and what has caused it, it's referring to what we can directly observe as the cause of excellence. This isn't about theorizing about what actions *might* have resulted in or contributed to a state of excellence. This is about cause and effect. What people, actions, places, and processes have contributed to your success? Visualize them and place them in your circle.

THEATER OF THE MIND

With real-life practice, some moves will be done excellently, but others less well. With mental practice, however, it is possible to repeat, in your mind, time after time, a move that you remember doing in the past. If the original move was really good, the imagined ones will be just as good. It seems that this repeated imagined activity stimulates nerve connections in the brain in the same way that real activities do. This sets up pathways for repeated excellence and, because there will be no errors in your mental activity, the repeated movements will enhance the skill when put into practice in real life—often more so than real-life practice.

NLP Made Easy, by Carol Harris (Element 2003), p. 101

If you're thinking that Theater of the Mind is characterized by visualization, you're correct. We must recognize the power of our imagination; it is 88% of our mind! The better you are at using your imagination, the more successful you'll be when you use Theater of the Mind later. Here's how it works:

- Make a movie of yourself. You're the director and you're also the star.
- Whenever you are called upon to use Theater of the Mind, either in one of the scripts or in one of the Perfect Enough CDs, you'll create the entire scene. What you look like, who's around you, what's around you, what kind of day it is, and what you are wearing will all be part of your movie. The object is to create as realistic a vision as possible of the outcome you'd like to achieve.
- Add as much sensory information as you can pack in to your

movie. It's 3-D, it's scratch and sniff, and you can even taste it.

- Remember to also add internal dialogue. In movies, there are voiceovers to tell us what the characters are thinking. What are your characters thinking? What are they feeling? How would you describe their inner lives?

Here are some tips for effective Theater of the Mind experiences:

- Learn to control your imagination. Practice visualizing. Imagine that your hands are lighter and lighter and your feet are heavier and heavier. It might sound like hocus pocus, but if you can master these exercises, you can affect your body with your mind. That skill is highly desirable—in fact vital—to success using Theater of the Mind and hypnosis.

- Learn to use your imagination when preparing for constructive activities, such as living your life with balance. The next time you're having a good time, pay close attention to everything around you. Attend to things you usually take for granted, like the color of the sky and the way things sound. Though these details may seem like minutiae, they'll be helpful later when you're creating one of your Theater of the Mind productions.

- Develop your creativity. Visualize new inventions, new services, new movies, new approaches to old problems and relationships.

- When your perception tells you you're up against a wall, let your imagination run wild. Brainstorm. Don't judge your ideas or edit them—just let them flow and associate freely.

- Practice and practice and practice until you are comfortable using your imagination easily and effectively.

ANCHORING

Anchoring is a technique that creates a response through the use of association. It's based on classical behavioral conditioning and involves creating a trigger that will be connected to a desired response. It completely bypasses your conscious and creates an instant reaction. The conscious mind can't stop the reaction you have programmed.

Anchors can be just about anything: a touch (e.g., when you touch your hair); a sight (e.g., when you see the refrigerator); or a complex set of movements (e.g., when you get up in front of a group of people with your PowerPoint materials and other props to give a presentation). The key is to attach the anchor to a desired emotional response. For example: when you stand at the podium, you immediately relax . . .

I've found that anchoring is the tool that creates the most powerful, lasting changes in my clients. I use it multiple times in all of my personal sessions and all of my CDs, and I recommend that you get comfortable with it and use it when you create self-hypnosis scripts of your own.

KNOW THYSELF!

Neuro-Linguistic Programming is a vehicle for self-knowledge that you can enlist everyday to help you achieve your goals. The more you know about yourself, the better you'll be able to plan your transformation and growth.

In addition, once you've observed someone else and you know how they look at the world, you're in a better position to effectively and efficiently communicate with them, as well. The more you know about someone, the better position you are in to predict their behavior. Think about it: You have two friends who are similar in a lot of ways and share many of the same interests. For instance, they both like to ski. However one prefers moguls while the other prefers cross-country skiing. Who do you think needs more stimulation?

Perhaps the most helpful aspect of NLP for hypnosis and self-hypnosis is to understand which sense you prefer to use when taking in and processing new information. Research has shown that most people are **visual, auditory,** or **kinesthetic.** Here are some quick tips on how to determine which one you are:

Visual people (55% of population) tend to focus on pictures, colors, sizes, angles, contrasts of focus, and brightness. They tend to talk fast, think in pictures and charts, and prefer to be *shown* how to do new things. They often speak of how they "see" things ("looks good to me," "I see what you mean," "the future is looking brighter"). They pay careful attention to their appearance and the appearance of others. Their respiration is shallow and quick. They use words like:

Appear	Look	See eye-to-eye
Clarity	Notice	Sketchy
Display	Peek	Stare
Focus	Peer	View
Hindsight	Probe	Watch
Illusion	Scene	Witness

Auditory people (21%) focus on words, volume, cadence, inflection, pauses, pitch, and tempo. They're good at handling people, are open to both sides of an argument, and like good questions. They think in language, talk about how things sound ("sounds good to me," "this rings a bell," "I'm all ears"), and dominate conversations. Background noises can either bug or help them. If you want them to do something, you should explain it to them (not show them or give them written instructions). They breathe deeply and speak rhythmically. They use words like:

Announce	Echo	Outspoken	Tongue-tied
Boisterous	Growl	Resonate	Utter
Confess	Howl	Screech	Vocal
Deafening	Mention	Speechless	Whisper

Kinesthetic people (24%) focus on feelings, texture, vibration, intensity, pressure, tension, and movement. What they perceive is often a reflection of their feelings. They touch people frequently, and they judge situations and people by how they make them feel inside ("that doesn't feel right to me," "she's so thin-skinned," "I have to dig deep for the answer"). They breathe deeply and slowly, are more patient than the other types, and they speak slower and lower. Because they take most of their cues from their feelings, they're more prone to moodiness. They use words like:

Burning	Heated	Relax	Stress
Caress	Lukewarm	Rush	Stroke
Euphoric	Muddled	Shift	Touch
Firm	Pressure	Solid	Unsettled

If you're still unsure of category you fit into, try this: Write a story about one of your fondest memories. A couple of paragraphs is all that's necessary. Aside from reliving an enjoyable moment, you'll be able to determine which of your faculties you tend to see your world through. Examine your verbiage. Which sense appears to be dominant in your story?

This will come in handy later when you create affirmations and self-hypnosis scripts for yourself, as their effectiveness is contingent upon how specifically and intensely they appeal to the lens you use to process new information.

Hypnosis and NLP are powerful tools when used properly and together. In the next chapter, I'll introduce "Laws" that dictate why and how things happen the way they do in our lives. When you factor these laws into the retraining of your brain, you can create meaningful change in any area of life you choose.

CHAPTER 3

THE LAWS OF THE UNIVERSE AND THE NATURAL LAWS OF THE MIND

The following laws came to me by way the amazing Dorothy Gates, Ph.D., whom I introduced in Chapter One. She was my mentor and my friend, and she saved my life. You'll find that the laws have a lot in common with philosophical and spiritual traditions that originated in the East and have been increasingly accepted in the West. Some of them were introduced in the United States during the New Age movement and were dismissed as "fluff," but since then plenty of evidence has been amassed that they're valid and not as whimsical, nonscientific, and "out there" as they once considered.

THE LAWS OF THE UNIVERSE

The Laws of the Universe are exactly what they sound like: they describe the way the universe—the energy of the universe—functions. Because they are laws, they are always true.

THE LAW OF ATTRACTION

We attract to us what we project out into the world through our thoughts, feelings, and actions. Like magnets, we send a powerful message about what we want, and we get it. The only problem is that most of us don't realize that's what we're doing.

Thoughts are energy, feelings are energy, and actions are energy, and *like attracts like,* meaning energy gravitates toward energy that is similar to it. Everyone's thoughts, feelings, and actions combined, in addition to everything that surrounds us, is the central engine of our being and our consciousness as a species. We are all part of the same energy field. It influences us, and we influence it in return. All things that are alike gather together; they attract each other. So if you are positive, you gather with other positive energies; you attract them. And if you are negative, you attract other negative energies. *What do you want to attract?* Whatever it is, begin by projecting it.

THE LAW OF CAUSE AND EFFECT

There can be no effect without a cause. Think about it. Things don't just happen—they're the results of your thoughts, actions and deeds. And in terms of your mind, as we saw in Chapter One, that means that your results are the 12%, but the causes can be found in the 88% of your mind. Therefore, though everything has a cause, it's likely that you might not know what that cause is. You need to tap into your huge 88% in order to create real, sustained change.

MY FAVORITE DOROTHY GATES-ISMS

Dorothy had dozens of great one-, two-, and even three-liners. Some of my favorite ones that pertain to The Law of Cause and Effect are:

- Every action in the universe must be followed by an appropriate reaction. There's no exception of any kind, at any time, for any reason.
- We get out of life what we put into life—no more and no less.
- If we make mistakes in life, we eventually pay the price. We are the arbiters of our own destiny.
- Thoughts we dwell upon in our minds are the seeds, and the seeds will create an entire harvest according to the law of 'like produces like.' All seeds must reproduce according to type. Seed determines the type, harvest reveals the seed sown.
- Having an *attitude of gratitude* is a vital part of creating your future, as you'll attract more of what you tell the universe you are grateful for. Sporadic moments of gratitude aren't enough; you must make a habit of continuously expressing and projecting how thankful you are.

Thanks to Dorothy, I have learned to use my energy to attract and create what I need for my own personal happiness and balance, and to her, I am eternally grateful.

THE LAW OF FREE THOUGHT

We can choose to use our free thought and free will for good or not, and we'll always face the consequences of our choices—sooner or later. We are the sum total of our choices.

Peace, plenty and security aren't detached from us; they aren't things that exist apart from us. In fact, they are inside of us, and if we choose to think and believe that's true, it will be true.

THE LAW OF WORK

We live in two spheres: vocational and personal. The wise person seeks to achieve harmony between the two. Our purpose is to make a contribution while we're here, and to advance the act of living to some degree by having lived. We should all be occupied in the highest employment our nature is capable of, and leave this lifetime with the consciousness that we've done our best. No one can ask more of you than that you do your best.

THE LAW OF HUMAN RELATIONS

Society is an extension of the individual. The first human unit is the individual, then the family, the community, the city, the nation, and the world. The contribution of every nation is the result of the quality of its citizens. So if you think your community, your state, or your nation needs improvement, you can be the starting point of that improvement. And in case you're thinking someone else will be the starting point, what if they're thinking that, too?

We owe it to ourselves and to each other to do what we can to promote peace and compassion. Remember that one warped mind affects everyone in the community. We've seen that time after time.

As Dr. Wayne Dyer writes in his book, *The Power of Intention* (Hay House 2004), "Be the peace you're seeking from others. . . . see the light in others, and treat them as if that is all you see" (169-70). If you need love, be love. If you need compassion, be compassion. Whatever it is you want from this life, be that first. And because like attracts like, you will attract what you need once you have *become* it.

THE LAW OF PERCEPTION

Every human being is the exact center of his own life and the way he thinks and feels has a direct and powerful influence upon the way he interacts with others as well as his environment. We see our world not as *it is,* but as *we are.* Whatever happens or occurs is always treated subjectively. It's impossible for any of us to be objective about our own lives.

Bestselling author Richard Carlson, Ph.D. discusses precisely this in *You Can Be Happy No Matter What: Five Principles for Keeping Life in Perspective* (New World 1997).

We have innocently learned to interpret our thoughts as if they were "reality," but thought is merely an ability that we have—we are the ones who produce the thoughts. It's easy to believe that because we think something, the object of our thinking (the content) represents reality (7).

THE LAW OF THE ETERNAL PRESENT

The subconscious is geared to act, react and respond in only one time period: now. Everything it does and everything it can do, it does now, in the present. The future is only your present expectation of something that may or may not become a reality.

As Eckhart Tolle writes in his bestseller *The Power of Now: A Guide to Spiritual Enlightenment* (New World 1999):

Nothing exists outside the Now. . . . What you think of as the past is a memory trace, stored in the mind, of a former Now. When you remember the past, you reactivate a memory trace—and you do so Now. The future is an imagined Now, a projection of the mind. When the future comes, it comes as the Now. When you think about the future, you do it now. Past and future obviously have no reality of their own (41).

THE LAW OF CHANGE

*Life is filled with changes. It's whether we can cope with those
changes or not that determines whether we will grow with the situation or be overcome by it . . .*
—Joan Borysenko, Ph.D., author of the bestseller, *Minding the
Body, Mending the Mind* (Bantam 1987), p. 23.

Our creativity and efficiency are directly related to our appetite for
change. It makes sense, then, that the inability to adapt to change causes
this natural appetite to atrophy. And the result is indecision, doubt,
fear and dullness. Meanwhile, if you embrace and are willing to adapt
to change, you stimulate the creative faculty of your subconscious. And
though none of us knows what is ahead, we do know that all things
pass away, and all things change. The important thing is to use today
wisely and well and face tomorrow eagerly and cheerfully.

It's also important to realize we aren't just passive victims of our
ever-changing world. We can create change if we desire to. In Louise
L. Hay's classic book, *You Can Heal Your Life* (Hay House 1987), she
discusses the process of change. She writes of the patterns that we all
have buried deep inside us, and that we must become aware of those
patterns in order to heal our overall condition. Becoming aware of our
patterns means accepting responsibility for creating the situations we
are involved in and learning what we need to learn.

Once you have acknowledged the past and learned from it, it's
time to release it and forgive whomever you believe has injured you.
And that includes yourself. I use a technique called Release and Clear,
which I'll outline later. As Louise Hay writes:

*The only thing you ever have any control over is your current thought . . . . Your
old thoughts are gone; there is nothing you can do about them except live out*

the experiences they caused. Your current thought, the one you are thinking right now, is totally under your control (66).

In other words, you are in complete control over if, when, and to what extent you will change. The power lies within you in your thoughts. You can use your thoughts to decide to change and then to create a new behavior that you can eventually transform into a habit.

The secret of handling our changing conditions is adapting to the Natural Laws of the Mind.

NATURAL LAWS OF THE MIND

The purpose of the Natural Laws of the Mind is to describe unequivocal truths about how our minds work. Once you embrace these truths, you're in a position to work *with* your mind, rather than against it. The law of electricity must be obeyed before it can become man's servant, right? When handled ignorantly, it becomes man's deadly foe. The same is true of Nature's laws. Similarly, although you might not know all of the details about how the law of electricity works, you know that it does work, and for most people, that's enough. You need only to be aware of the Natural Laws of the Mind—not how they work. Leave that part to Nature.

LAW #1
WHAT YOU THINK IS WHAT YOU GET.

Any image placed into the subconscious mind develops into reality with absolute accuracy. Life is formed from the inside out; it's not determined by outward acts or circumstances. It should make sense, then, that each of us creates our own life with our thoughts. A single thought will neither make nor break a life; but a habit of thought will. You cannot think defeat and be victorious; it's impossible.

The subconscious mind responds only to mental images. It doesn't matter if the image is self-induced or from the external world. The mental image formed becomes the blueprint and the subconscious mind uses every means at its disposal to carry out the plan. Because that's true, an activity or behavior such as worrying would be the programming of an image you don't want. The subconscious, not knowing the difference between a real or imagined image, will act to fulfill the imagined situation and the things you fear most are more likely to happen.

As Wayne Dyer wrote in *Manifest Your Destiny*:

If your mental pictures are of being surrounded by things and conditions that you desire, and they are rooted in joy and faith, your creative thoughts will attract these surroundings and conditions into your life. . . . What you are doing is literally visualizing in detail what it is that you want to manifest . . . . You detach from the outcome and how it will be accomplished. You are not in the business of creating, but of attracting to yourself what is already in creation . . . (p. 60).

When you change your thoughts, you change your mind.

Law #2
Every thought causes a physical reaction.

Our power of creation is the word. The word is the most powerful tool that humans possess. It is the tool of magic.
Don Miguel Ruiz, *The Four Agreements Companion Book*
(Amber Allen, 2000).

Your thoughts affect all of the functions of your body. For example:

- Worry thoughts trigger changes in the stomach that eventually lead to ulcers.
- Anger thoughts stimulate your adrenal glands and the increased adrenaline in the bloodstream causes many other physical changes.
- Anxiety and fear thoughts change your pulse rate.
- Hunger and thirst thoughts affect your stomach and salivary glands.
- Sex thoughts affect your sex organs.

Though personal body chemistry is guided and triggered by your emotions, it is your thought that leads the emotions. You can actually make yourself sick, poor and unhappy, just by thinking the wrong thoughts habitually. It's a law that *you become what you dwell upon.*

The best way to instantly grasp Law #2 is The Lemon Test. Read the following a couple of times until you have committed the short process to memory. Then, close your eyes and see what happens!

Imagine you are in your kitchen on a bright, sunny day. Look around you and notice the colors and the light in the room.

Slowly work your way to the refrigerator, noticing everything along the way. Notice which way the door to the refrigerator opens. When you open the door you notice a lemon on the shelf in front of you. Look at a lemon. Feel it. Pick it up, bring it to a cutting board next to the sink, and pick up the sharp knife lying next to the cutting board. Slice the bright, yellow lemon in half. Imagine yourself smelling the lemon, bringing it to your mouth, and then squeezing some of the juice onto your tongue.

Did you salivate? Did your mouth pucker? Did you notice a taste that reminded you of something? Through your thoughts about the lemon, you created a physical reaction. Isn't it amazing how easy it is?

LAW #3
IMAGINATION IS MORE POWERFUL THAN KNOWLEDGE.

Images are the property of the subconscious mind (that huge 88% of your brain we discussed in Chapter One). Those images will always overpower what you think (the scant 12%). Reason is easily overruled by imagination. In fact, an idea accompanied by a strong emotion usually cannot be modified through the use of reason. However, by subconscious reprogramming, any idea can be easily and effortlessly removed, altered, or amended.

The way I teach my clients about this Natural Law of the Mind is I say: "Look at me right now. I am wearing a white shirt and navy-blue trousers, right? Okay, now close your eyes and picture me with a green shirt and purple trousers and a black hat."

"Now open your eyes and tell me which is real." Your mind doesn't know, as it has seen both and cannot tell the difference.

LAW #4
YOUR HABITS ARE YOUR LIFE.

Life is full of habits. Much of your day consists of successions of actions that have become more or less automatic. Ninety-seven percent of what we do, we do by habit, spontaneously. Each separate act (habit), good or bad, plays a part in making you what you are. Fortunately, it's never too late, and you're never too old, to change your habits. You can begin today. You can begin right now, at this very moment. Remember that success is a habit and so is failure. Repetition forms positive habits and negative ones.

> *Men do little from reason, much from passion, most from habit.*
> —Dorothy Gates, Ph.D.

YOU CAN FORETELL YOUR FUTURE

A surefire way to tell what your future will hold is to look at your habits of today. If you don't change any of your habits of today, there's one place they'll inevitably lead you. For example, if you have a habit of plateau-ing at a certain weight every time you try a new diet, and you are aware of that plateau and remind yourself of that plateau, thereby giving a lot of energy and reinforcement to it, I guarantee you that the next time you try to lose weight, you will plateau at the same number.

Furthermore, if you believe you can lose weight only by exercising, I guarantee you will lose weight only by exercising. Lucky for me, I didn't believe that one, and I lost twenty-five pounds by eating real food and stopping when I felt full. And I didn't exercise once.

YOUR HABITS DON'T CHANGE BY THEMSELVES; YOU HAVE TO DO THE WORK.

If you could change by just reading a book about change or going to therapy, everyone would be replacing all of their negative thoughts and behavior with positive ones. But it's not that easy. Reading doesn't create change easily or automatically. You need something more. Extinguishing bad habits involves cultivating new ones. And that work has to be on the subconscious level.

One of the things you need to do to change a behavior is repetition. What you use increases, and what you don't use will atrophy from lack of use. All of your talents increase or decrease in proportion to the extent to which you apply them. Once a habit is formed, it becomes easier and easier to follow and more difficult to break.

In bestselling author Napoleon Hill's *Keys to Success: The 17 Principles of Personal Achievement* (Plume 1994), he refers to "The Three Essentials of Cosmic Habitforce" (209-212). What he's really talking about is how and why we form habits. The first essential is "plasticity," which is simply the ability to change that is part of our make up. The second is "frequency of impression," which means that the more you do something the faster it becomes a habit. "Repetition is the mother of habit," Hill writes.

Finally, "intensity of impression" is the third essential and means that the more concentration involved in doing something, the faster it will become a habit. "You impress the habit on your subconscious mind, and it becomes a part of everything you do."

LAW #5
DON'T BREED NEGATIVE THOUGHTS.

As you probably have learned through experience, the more attention and power you give your fears, the more they affect you and the more likely they are to manifest themselves. If you continue to fear ill health, constantly talk about your "nerves," "tension headaches," "nervous stomach," in time those changes will occur, and do so quite naturally. Your nerves will act up, you'll get tension headaches, and you will experience stomach problems. All because you kept those negative notions in your mind.

This is true with any negative thought. The more you concentrate on your failures in relationships, the more likely you are to fail (in similar ways) in future relationships. In general, the more you allow fear and other negative thoughts to invade your life, the stronger their presence will become. And once they are firmly entrenched in your mind, your body will begin to create behavior to support them. You will supply physical, emotional, and mental behaviors and experiences to support the negativity you attend to.

LAW #6
ATTITUDE IS A MATTER OF CHOICE.

You cannot control the external circumstances of your life, but you can control your reactions to them.
—Joan Borysenko, Ph.D., *Minding the Body, Mending the Mind* (Bantam 1988, p. 207).

An attitude is the way you look at life, and as we've all experienced, attitudes affect the body and how it performs. Fortunately, we all have the innate ability to choose our attitude in any given set of circumstances.

The events that occur in our lives are purely neutral. They're not positive until we've decided they are, and they're not negative until we've decided they are. For example, I can decide to view the death of a loved one as a negative event. But death is a part of life, and perhaps that loved one's purpose had been fulfilled and now they are in a much better situation than being human on Planet Earth. When I look at it that way, I can choose to view the death as a neutral event.

In NLP, when we refer to "reframing," we are talking about the ability we all have to shift our perspective, and in turn change our approach and probably change the outcome. So the death of a loved one might, on some level be cause for grief. But it also might be cause for giving thanks. It depends on how you look at it.

Law #7
REACTIONS MUST BE MANAGED.

This law is the corollary to the previous one. Just as you can manage your attitude, you can manage your reactions. Again, what happens in your life is purely neutral. But how you react to what happens is not; it can affect your health, your relationships, and your career.

One of the more prevalent problems my clients have is the inability to handle themselves in a situation that is not comfortable for them. For instance, road rage comes up often. What do you do when you're driving along and someone cuts you off? If you are in the mindset to be angry in that nanosecond, a response of anger and aggression such as yelling, cussing, or swearing happens instantly. To be able to manage yourself is to understand why you would ever respond in such a negative, counter-productive way. Have you seen a parent or a significant other act so disproportionately angry? Have you seen the expression of road rage in a movie? Is that what you're recreating? Where did you learn your road rage? What was the anchor—the cue— that "made you" respond with road rage? Was it a car horn? A car not accelerating within a moment of a light turning green? Someone cutting you off? Once you determine what is the most common anchor for your road rage, all you have to do is reprogram the way you react to that anchor.

All feelings are good, because their purpose is to
provide us with information, direction, and motivation
that will help us create a satisfying life.
—Calvin D. Banyan

Law #8

Thoughts must be kept alive.

Every thought you have must be fed and nurtured in order to keep it alive. And when your conscious mind has recognized an idea as true and guiding, it cannot simultaneously hold an opposing thought. In other words, only one idea can be entertained at one time. For example, let's say an individual believes in absolute integrity. He trains and expects his children to be honest, and he expects everyone he does business with to be honest. Meanwhile, he cheats on his income taxes. He might rationalize his conduct by saying, "Everybody else does it." He cannot, however, escape the conflict and its effect upon his nervous system that is caused by attempting to hold opposing ideas.

The following are truisms about your thoughts:

- An idea, once accepted, tends to remain until it's replaced by another idea or it's forgotten.
- Once an idea has been accepted, there's opposition to replacing it with a new idea.
- The longer an idea remains, the more opposition there is to replacing it with a new idea.
- The longer an idea remains, the more it tends to become a fixed habit of thinking. (This is how habits are formed, both good and bad ones: first the thought, then the action.)
- Therefore, if we wish to change our actions, we must begin by changing our thoughts.

Law #9

Have an attitude of gratitude.

What you put forth comes back to you—and usually when it does it has gained mass and momentum. This is true of the way you treat people and even the way you deal with money. In other words, what goes around comes around. Therefore, if you develop an attitude of gratitude, and you look at your life in terms of all you have to be grateful for, you'll start seeing more to be grateful for, focusing on positive things, and more positive things will then be attracted to you.

In *Manifest Your Destiny* (Harper Collins 1997) Dr. Wayne Dyer writes, "The nature of gratitude helps dispel the idea that we do not have enough, that we will never have enough, and that we ourselves are not enough. . . . Gratitude is a way of experiencing the world with love rather than judgment" (149-50).

PART II
THE 8 KEYS TO DISCOVER

CHAPTER 4

KEY #1: SELF-CONFIDENCE

FROM INSECURE TO EMPOWERED

*You gain strength, courage and confidence by every experience in
which you really stop to look fear in the face.*
—Eleanor Roosevelt

con fi dence (kon - fi - d*uh* ns)
noun

1. full trust; belief in the powers, trustworthiness, or reliability of a
   person or thing: *We have every confidence in their ability to succeed.*
2. belief in oneself and one's powers or abilities; self-confidence; self-
   reliance; assurance: *His lack of confidence defeated him.*

   Dictionary.com. *Dictionary.com Unabridged (v 1.0.1)*, Based on the Random House
   Unabridged Dictionary, © Random House, Inc. 2006.

IF YOU HAVE SELF-CONFIDENCE, you have a firm
belief in your powers, abilities, or capacities. And if you don't, you
might be perfectly capable, successful person, but one or more of the
following fears might be keeping you from believing in yourself.

- The fear of being yourself:
  - o Maybe others won't like you.
  - o Maybe others won't value you.
- The fear of not being yourself:
  - o You were put on this Earth to do something/be someone. What if you don't fulfill that destiny?
- The fear of making mistakes:
  - o What if others criticize you?
  - o If you make a mistake, that means you're not perfect.

Fear is a painful emotion triggered by the apprehension of (real or imagined) danger, terror, or displeasure. I say real or imagined because many of our fears are merely concoctions of our imagination. But as I've said, your subconscious mind cannot distinguish between real images and imagined ones. It will produce the same fear response throughout the body for both. And then, as you probably know by now, what you fear is then likely to become your reality.

HOW DOES FEAR AFFECT YOU PHYSICALLY?

Once the mind gets the signal that there is something to fear (whether or not there is, in reality), it releases hormones throughout the body that trigger defensive chemical mechanisms. This is the "fight, flight or fright" response we've all heard about and experienced.

- A message is sent to your hypothalamus, which regulates the stress response, to be on high alert.
- Your hypothalamus sends out signals preparing you for your response.
- Within nanoseconds, blood rushes to the center of your body, increasing your heart rate and your blood pressure, and then your muscles tense.

- Your hands and feet get cold and sweaty, and you're ready to fight—or flee.
- Fear stimulates chemical releases in the brain that block thinking and concentration and immobilize you. Fear can make you completely freeze.
- If you are in the presence of something that could realistically cause you physical harm, you have anywhere from a few seconds to a few minutes to respond, and either flee or defend yourself.

CONQUERING FEAR

To overcome your fear, you must first identify where and when you learned it. Is it rational? Irrational? Either way, it is real to you in your mind, and sometimes once you acknowledge the origin as irrational, it becomes easier to overcome.

Whether your fear is of a past experience recurring or of something new, that fear tends to be relived over and over again until it has snowballed to such a point that it is all-consuming.

You might think that I'm going to help you eliminate your fear, but actually there is no such thing. Instead, we aim for releasing it and replacing it with a positive reaction to the very same stimuli. I like to think of it as mastering your fear. As Mark Twain once said, *"Courage is resistance to and mastery of fear—not the absence of fear."* In order to master your fear, you must identify it and get to know it well.

EXERCISES TO HELP YOU MASTER YOUR FEARS

• WRITE YOUR *FEAR PROFILE*

Everyone should begin here and do this exercise at least once with each of their fears. Give your fear a name and write its biography.

When did it come into your life? Why? Describe the day, if you recall, and/or the circumstance. Like when you are doing a Theater of the Mind exercise, compose a story with rich sensory details. Often the mere creation and writing of the story deepens your understanding of your fear and helps you master it. Remember, you cannot master something if you don't know it well.

• INSTANT CHANGE OF STATE

The instant an unpleasant thought enters your mind simply assure yourself that "The most powerful experience of this moment is the relaxation I am feeling." When you say this, you are diminishing the power of the fear and its effect on you. You are taken to a place of safety and serenity so your body can use its precious resources on the task at hand rather than on overreacting.

Face your fears slowly to desensitize yourself to their effects. And repeat your exposure to them over and over until you realize that the dread in your head is much greater than the actual potential for harm.

• BREATH

The in-breath followed by the out-breath represents tension and release. And when the breath is blocked, the body and mind are blocked and in a state of substandard performance. There must be freely flowing breath in order for peak performance and true contentment to exist. When you disconnect from your breath, you prevent flow, and you create tension that is at cross-purposes with the balance and happiness you're working to achieve.

• BLOWING YOUR FEARS AWAY

Find a quiet place and breathe deeply, slowly, and completely.

Visualize the thing, event, or person that is at the center of your biggest fear. See everything about the moment you fear most, and then add more sensory details. Feel that moment of your biggest fear. Smell it. Hear it. Then . . . shrink it. Continue to shrink the image in your mind until it's so small that when you hold it in the palm of your hand you can barely see, feel, smell, or hear it.

Then . . . blow on it once, and send it off into oblivion, never to return.

When you face your fears you quickly and easily move into the realm of security, trust, and confidence in your own abilities. And included in those abilities, is the capacity you have to change your life and reach your potential.

If you don't have self-confidence, the odds are that you won't be positioned to attract love, find meaning, get healthy, or improve your life in any other way. And you certainly won't have what it takes to persevere through whatever trials life brings your way. Your capacity to discover your true self and believe that you are Perfect Enough can be traced to one core concept: self-confidence. That's what you need to develop first. And luckily, it's not that hard.

Do you know anyone who has a high level of self-confidence? How does it manifest? Usually, when we see people who "Just do it" we attribute that ability to jump right in to their self-confidence. They might make dozens of mistakes, but they're not afraid of mistakes, so mistakes don't faze them. Self-confident individuals take advantage of opportunities to act, rather than make excuses why they shouldn't act. And they probably fail more often than other people, but that's because they act more often than other people.

It's important to distinguish between confidence and competence. There are many people who are successful and have reached a high level of competence. But that doesn't mean they have confidence in their abilities. On the other hand, there is such a thing as too much confidence. Overconfidence is as dangerous as lack of confidence, and often produces a similar result: failure. Too much confidence can mislead you into thinking that you have competence that you don't really have.

WHY IT'S GOOD TO BE SELFISH

The core of self-confidence is self-love. And for all of us, that is developed in childhood. Did your parents exhibit confidence? How was confidence modeled to you when you were a child? Would you describe your parents as people who loved themselves? If so, how did that love manifest itself?

I have found that people who find it difficult to love themselves often have one thing in common: they learned to equate self-love with selfishness.

self ish (sel fish)
adjective
1. devoted to or caring only for oneself; concerned primarily with one's own interests, benefits, welfare, etc., regardless of others.
    selfish. Dictionary.com. *Dictionary.com Unabridged (v 1.0.1)*.
    Random House, Inc. http://dictionary.reference.com/browse/selfish (accessed: December 16, 2006).

Once we have been taught to NOT be selfish, the subconscious mind, because it's so literal, makes sure you don't spend any (or too much) time taking care of yourself. Every single time, the end result is that the true person gets lost in the sauce. If your core value structure is built on not caring supremely for yourself, you are literally telling yourself to leave yourself out of the realm of caring. Everyone else is allowed attention and love, yet you get left behind.

At some point in adulthood, many people turn to self-help products when they realize they haven't been taking care of themselves. They read books, listen to tapes and CDs, and feed themselves information—on a conscious level—that doesn't jibe with what is in their subconscious mind. They soon begin searching for comfort because they are confused and don't even know it. Some find comfort in alcohol, some in drugs, and yet others in more socially-acceptable compulsive behaviors, such as obsessing over their appearance and becoming addicted to cosmetic surgery. Some decide that an anti-depressant is necessary. I'm not here to put down the use of the magic pills that I always see bouncing across my television screen. But I *am* here to say there is another way to feel better: another way to feel *good*.

If you want to make changes in your life, you first must see yourself as whole. You are not broken. However, you haven't developed a map in your mind that tells you that you are worthy of being loved. You have a different map, and regardless of what or whom you are surrounded by, your map tells you that there's something wrong with you.

As I sit here and type, I too have little voices that had come from my past that I must cancel and replace with more positive thoughts. My little voices tell me that I'm not very smart. I have spent my life striving to be the best I can be. I have gone to many classes, I'm a voracious reader, and I practice what I have learned—and I now teach—on a daily basis. What I haven't told you is that when I was a young girl I had a teacher who spent an entire year telling me I wasn't smart. That created a map in my brain that told me I would have to keep learning and learning and learning in an attempt to be smart.

I can reframe what my teacher used to say to me and conclude: That map helped me become successful because I was driven to learn. And that's true. However, that map also created a lack of confidence. I wasn't learning because I loved to learn and it made me feel good; I was learning because I thought I needed to be fixed.

As you might imagine, when a person in your life has contributed to a map that doesn't work in your best interest, part of your new and improved map must include forgiving that person. Forgiveness is a part of every spiritual tradition, as is the notion that God loves you regardless of your flaws. And if you're good enough for God to love and forgive, you should be good enough for yourself to love and forgive.

It is sometimes unbelievable the things God has sent my way. Thirty-two years ago, hypnosis saved my life. I had a lot of issues that created a negative self-image and profound feelings of unworthiness and depression. My parents did everything they thought was helpful, including sending me to an inpatient mental rehabilitation center. I took the correct medication and did a good job with the therapy, which at that time was all on the conscious level. After moving forward in life successfully for a bit, the depression came back. By that time, my mother had heard about hypnosis and had discovered Dorothy Gates, who saved my life, and to whom I dedicated my first book, *The Power to Win* (Lyons 2004). She passed away eight years ago and I still miss her. It is because of Dorothy and the possibilities she opened up to me that I am a certified hypnotist. Remember, one of the presuppositions of NLP is that if one person can do something, you can too.

WE ARE BOMBARDED WITH REASONS TO FEEL INSECURE

When you're standing in a grocery store line, your subconscious mind is picking up all the messages from the magazines around you. What are the images? Most are beautiful, thin movie stars, right? Your brain takes in all those tall, skinny, perfectly-coiffed beauties, and saves it as the programming for "what I need to be." Then, naturally, those images are juxtaposed with the reality of how you look, and guess what?

You don't compare. But it doesn't stop there. You then conjure up a feeling of discomfort about yourself that manifests both mentally ("I'm fat") and physically (you actually *feel* bad about yourself). And worst of all, you don't realize that you allowed all of that to occur.

This happens not only in the grocery store, but when you're watching television and when you're at the movies. You are programmed with images of what you should look like, and you are left feeling unattractive, overweight, and insecure. You are even barraged with images of impossibly romantic relationships, and when you compare your relationships to them, you fail miserably. Remember, the subconscious mind doesn't have the ability to analyze or rationalize the information. It doesn't say, "Sure all those movie stars are thin and have perfect skin and hair. It often takes hours to get them to look like that, and they get paid to look good, so they often spend a lot of money on skin treatments, hair treatments, personal trainers, and personal chefs. Heck, if I had all that, I'd look great and attract Mr. Perfect, too!" That doesn't occur in the subconscious. All that happens is the images are catalogued as "expected appearance" and "expected relationship," and you're stuck in a hopeless position where you can be never thin enough, tall enough, or attractive enough. Position yourself to say, *I look great and I'm married to Mr. Fabulous because I use my **DISCOVER PROCESS** to create a happy, balanced life!*

TOP 10 REASONS TO DISLIKE YOURSELF

Most people don't need any help finding things to dislike about themselves, so the following aren't suggestions, but are a comforting reality. Most people have at least a few of them, and if you've got most of them, you're not alone. My experience as a hypnotherapist has shown me that the following are the top ten reasons people dislike themselves. Check the ones that pertain to you.

1. You're not thin enough   ____
2. You're too short/tall   ____
3. You're not attractive   ____
4. You're never going to do well   ____
5. You can't make friends   ____
6. You worry about everything   ____
7. You don't like your work   ____
8. You're always waiting for the bad to happen   ____
9. You're never going to meet someone   ____
10. You're not smart enough   ____

The good news is that you've decided that it's time to turn them around or replace them with positive, productive feelings. One of my favorite ways to do this is by modeling.

ACTION STEP

MODELING SELF-CONFIDENCE

The impression we have of who we are and what we might be able to achieve is developed very early in life (many experts say by the age of nine, and certainly under the influence of our families). Fortunately, no matter what was planted in your mind regarding who you are and what your capable of (or incapable of) when you were a child, your self-image can be recreated.

Follow these steps to transform your negative self-image into a positive one, and improve your self-confidence:

1. Acknowledge that your self-image is negative and in need of change. Like your realization that your attitude about

mistakes needs adjusting, this is the crucial first step in the transformation of your confidence.

2. Evaluate yourself.

    a. Make a list of things you don't like about yourself that cannot be changed. (And then don't spend any more time trying to change them.)

    b. Make a list of things you like about yourself and what you're doing. *Notice how rereading the items you like about yourself boosts your confidence with each read. Add items each day and reread the entire list each day.*

    c. Make a list of things you don't like that CAN be changed. (Now here's a great place to focus some energy!)

3. Create a plan for changing the items in 2c.

How?

By modeling self-confidence.

- Who represents self-confidence to you?
- Close your eyes and imagine that person.
- Envision how the person stands, how they walk, and how they use their hands and eyes.
- Imagine that person interacting with others. What does their voice sound like? What do they look like when they're listening? Observe how the other people react to your confident person.
- Imagine yourself standing close to your confident person. How do you feel? Can you feel their confidence?
- Pretend you're a human sponge and soak up the self-confidence of your model.
- Turn to the people in your vision and watch them react to you the same way they reacted to your confident person.

Feel their respect and admiration, and feel your charisma and confidence.

- Now, open your eyes.

ACTION STEP

FILL-IN SECTION #1 OF YOUR DISCOVER OUTCOME DEVELOPMENT BOARD

Cut out and paste photos and words that represent your model of self-confidence onto section #1 of the Outcome Development Board from your Toolkit. If you don't have the Toolkit, simply use a poster-size piece of cardboard or construction paper, divided into eight sections (hold it horizontally and create four boxes on top and four on the bottom. Section #1 is the top left section.). You're creating a story with your board. The story begins with "I Am," and it should include every wonderful thing you already are as well as what you want your outcomes to be. Here are some tips for choosing the most effective images:

- Look for images of the body you would like to have, but keep it realistic for your height and body type.
- Look for pictures of people with the facial expressions and posture similar to the person you modeled in previous Action Step.
- Look for pictures of people who are dressed in a way that represents self-confidence to you.

Post your Board someplace where your conscious mind will continually see it. If your conscious mind sees it, your subconscious definitely does, too. And it's your subconscious that will use it to reprogram your mind.

ACTION STEP

Use Hypnosis to Turbo-charge Your New Self-Confidence

When you have a poor self-image, your first job is to recognize it. Then, in order to successfully develop a healthier, more positive self-image, you must release the negative one to make room for the new one. As with any self-hypnosis script, you must relax yourself first by using Instant Alpha Conditioning. Next, follow with the "Release and Clear" script to clear out negative thoughts, memories, or other images that creep into your mind and invade your thinking. This makes your brain available for more productive things. Once you have done the "Release and Clear" script 21 times, proceed to the "Self Confidence" script. *Remember to read the Instant Alpha Conditioning script before any self-hypnosis script.*

Let's get rid of your self-sabotaging thoughts and replace them with positive messages of Self-Confidence!

INSTANT ALPHA CONDITIONING

Instructions:

1. Use the word you selected to replace the longer Alpha conditioning script. Read the following script and let Alpha occur.

2. Proceed directly to the script for Release and Clear, and read each night, before retiring, for 21 nights. Read aloud, with feeling.

S	M	T	W	Th	F	Sat

3.   Say the words Release and Clear every night thereafter.

From this moment on, each and every time I desire to attain the deep state of total relaxation, I am instantly and fully relaxed, as I am now drifting into the Alpha state of consciousness. The moment I think my chosen word _____, Alpha occurs. This word has an effect only when I use it and only under the proper circumstances. Each and every time I do use it, I am fully prepared to receive positive, beneficial and constructive suggestions, impressing each one deeper into my storage and memory facility of my brain.

From this moment on, _____ triggers deep relaxation of my mind and body. I feel Alpha occur. I feel wonderful. I feel comfortable. I am totally receptive and responsive to my own creative ideas and suggestions. I am bathed in a glow of quietness, peace, and serenity. My chosen word works only when I deliberately use it for deep relaxation to attain Alpha consciousness. Its use in regular conversation has no effect on me whatsoever. From this moment on, each and every time I desire the deep state of total relaxation, I am instantly and fully relaxed upon saying _____. Because my subconscious must follow my command, each and every time I desire total relaxation, I am instantly and fully relaxed when I think my chosen word_____ _____. I feel a deep sense of gratification as this word programming becomes a reality. Feeling wonderful, generous, alive, and eager to Release and Clear my negative self-image . . .

RELEASE AND CLEAR

So relaxed . . . so relaxed . . . slowly drifting into a most satisfying state of relaxation. Relaxation is good for me. I release every last ounce of useless tension . . . as I rest contentedly, to awaken when I must, refreshed and invigorated. I am alive with the feeling of freedom, of promise, of exhilarating positive expectation. My mind is clear . . . my body recharged . . . and my past deactivated . . . and left behind me.

As I relax . . . I release every unhappy experience of the past . . . and everything connected with those experiences. I find it easy to let them go. I am a part of life . . . as are we all . . . and we all move, live, and think, as we have a right to. Life goes on, and so do I . . . growing rich in experience . . . and in capacity to achieve. My positive experiences supply me with a directness to meet the challenges of my life. All I must do is use the amazing power of my subconscious mind. I am using that capacity now to disengage me from every negative . . . destructive . . . and harmful impression ever made upon me. They fade . . . fade . . . fade out of my life forever.

I am grateful and thankful for every experience of the past. I now forgive myself for every mistake I have ever made; and I forgive everyone else who may have in any way harmed me. I know that out of each experience . . . as I understand it . . . good must surely come to me. I forgive myself for every mistake because I know that each mistake is a stepping-stone to greater understanding . . . to greater opportunity . . . and to greater achievement. I grow stronger with each experience . . . and I am stronger than anything life can offer. I am preparing myself to meet its challenges directly . . . free of negative conditioning. I am more than any challenge . . . for I possess the power and the ability to channel any experience into a rich and rewarding way of life.

I now fully release the past . . . and all its effects upon me. I am free . . . free of the past . . . free to be me . . . entirely. I accept myself completely. I am a valuable and talented human being . . . I am always aware of my innate worth. There are things to be done by me . . . that are done better by me than by any other human being. Every word . . . every movement . . . every gesture of mine . . . preserves my unique stamp upon life. For as long as time has been . . . or ever shall be .

. . there is no one who can exactly duplicate me. I am pleased . . . I accept myself . . . I love myself . . . I am grateful for my new level of understanding. My acceptance releases me from negative self-dislike . . . and so I am now free to change that which must be changed . . . to improve that which can be improved . . . to let go of that which is inhibiting or destructive. My self-acceptance now enables me to accept everyone else . . . I accept myself . . . I accept others as they are . . . I accept even those who are unacceptable . . . as unacceptable . . . and go on my way.

I bestow upon others my affection . . . true and unencumbered. In my imagination . . . I see them having all the good I desire for myself. What I desire for myself, I also desire for everyone else . . . I have fulfilled my nature. I have supplied myself with those priceless qualities and feelings . . . acceptance . . . love . . . and forgiveness . . . and so I now have them to give. I give them freely. I feel the warmth and excitement of building a new and rewarding life. A firm, quiet sense of self-love and self-determination dominates my every waking and sleeping hour. I am ready to release, and do so this night. CLEAR . . . CLEAR . . . CLEAR.

After you have done Release and Clear Script:
1.   Remain in a relaxed state,
2.   repeat your chosen alpha word, and
3.   proceed to the following script for self-confidence.

SELF-CONFIDENCE SCRIPT

This simple act of relaxation is instruction to my deeper level of mind. To repair. To revitalize my mental thoughts to be positive and allow me to be self-confident. Now I choose to relax and let it happen. Feel safe and secure. Let go. I relax deeper and deeper. Deeper and deeper. Somewhere in my deeper awareness is my blueprint of myself as a living being. I am programming my ability to duplicate this blueprint as new cells replace the old with positive self-confidence. With guidance my mind replaces them in the positive conditioned way. In a pattern which will work well for me now and in the future.

The reason I am reading this relaxation session is that I want to release all negative emotions of anxiety and worry that relate to my self-confidence. I have made a decision to be in control of my life and my thoughts. I have decided to enjoy life and be self-confident. That's right! Great. Now I am going to do a repeat technique that will build my own internal blueprint for confidences. I am going to say the following phrase with a lot of energy and excitement. I will repeat the phrase in a very special way, silently to myself, in the privacy of my own mind so I can hear the excitement as my own reality. Each time I say the phrase, I will say it with more energy and excitement because I know it is my reality and that is exciting.

"I am confident, strong and brave today and for the rest of my life."
"I am confident, strong and brave today and for the rest of my life."
"I am confident, strong and brave today and for the rest of my life."
"I am confident, strong and brave today and for the rest of my life."

I now instruct my deeper mind to replace and renew my old pattern concerning self-confidence with a new instruction to release the old pattern. To deliver to myself a new pattern following the guidelines presented here and now. I now impress my deeper awareness with a definite mental image of dynamic self-confidence. I accept myself as a lovable person with the ability to express and receive love. I am unique. I have special qualifications. There are things for me to do that are done better by me than by any other person.

I am important to life. I live in such a way that I approve of myself. I have confidence in my own judgment. I am honest and dependable.

My integrity is felt by everyone I meet. Through my creative thinking I now direct my life into wholesome and complete expression. I see myself expressing radiant vitality and boundless energy. I have the power to control my thoughts and direct them toward constructive and wise decisions. I have the courage and faith in myself to act with complete confidence. Within myself is a storehouse of untapped vitality, strength and courage. I now have faith in myself as I rely on this new self-confident power.

I find abundant courage and confidence in myself. As I reach a new dimension, many new doors open to me. Opportunities stimulate me to achieve much more satisfaction than I have ever experienced before. I soon recognize this dynamic change in my character and develop a new appreciation and respect for myself. I have faith and believe in myself. I am considerate and gentle to my loved ones and share my rewards generously. I am an individual who desires the finest life has to offer. My conscious thoughts inspire the way I find my own intention for life.

I am aware of these thoughts. They are becoming increasingly positive and helpful to my well-being. My deeper mind now supplies the means to fulfill all of my suggestions. I realize that genuine understanding and confidence in my uniqueness is a matter of gradual growth and development. As I faithfully plant the seeds of trust, of confidence in myself, my ability to express in my own unique way increases constantly. I enjoy the deep satisfaction of a now peaceful and enriching life. I now deeply impress my deeper mind with a mental image of dynamic self-confidence.

I demand of myself complete expression earnestly and sincerely believing in myself to be strong, brave, courageous, successful and self-confident.

I realize that I now have the power to express self-confidence, so that it acts as a powerful magnet to attract success and confidence in myself. Now allowing the law of attraction to be activated and strong within me toward what I truly want. My thoughts go directly toward what I want most. I favorably influence all persons with my positive inner attitude. I project feelings of cooperation to people, and my belief in myself is evident to all around me. My attitude toward people is helpful and cooperative, and I know that this positive attitude brings me success and happiness. I know that my self-confidence is increased by thinking power-generating thoughts. I think of myself as strong, resourceful, and self-reliant. I now have an inner consciousness of myself as agreeable, graceful, and pleasant. I have a genuine interest in others, which in turn increases my self-assurance. I sincerely enjoy communicating with others. Listening, speaking with assurance. The quality of my voice expresses power, self-confidence, and caring, and I have a well-modulated tone that expresses a positive and self-controlled person. All of my actions express my confident attitude. My eyes are straightforward. My body posture reflects confidence. My manner of walking is brisk and energetic.

I accept myself as a lovable person with the ability to express and receive love. I am unique. My positive thoughts generate positive energy around me. I choose my thoughts with a positive attitude. Directing them toward all positive feelings and then listening to my feelings. I attract positive energy from all around me. I have special qualifications. There are things for me to do that are done better by me than by any other person.

I respect myself and I realize that people accept me and highly regard me. I have a high and honest opinion of myself, and I expect respect and consideration from all people. People believe in me because I now believe in myself and in my power to achieve. I continuously grow in self-confidence, courage, and strength. Because I express my inner power by dynamic action, I realize a bright new life, full of personal achievement. I quietly accept the wonderful knowledge that I now express my highest ideal. I am dynamic. I believe in myself. I have dynamic self-confidence. I can and do achieve easily and effectively all that is in my best interest for my highest good.

This entire suggestion is represented by the color yellow. Yellow symbolizes strength and power to achieve my outcomes. My outcome is a self-confident me. And I now feel the strength and power flowing into my body and mind. I feel the golden yellow color filling my veins with self-confidence. And I am pleased. I continue to have unwavering faith. I keep faithfully planting the seeds of self-confidence. I secure the knowledge and my deeper awareness carries them out for me according to my instructions, my ability to express these new instructions is now increased and I enjoy the deep quiet satisfaction of a new, peaceful, self-confident life. Every time I see yellow, whether consciously or subconsciously, this session is doubled in my subconscious mind, allowing it to have the maximal potential in my life.

This entire suggestion is represented by the letter "D" of my sub-key word "Discover." Anytime I think, say, or see the word "Discover," all suggestions keyed to this word are automatically activated, stimulated and work for my benefit.

You now have the choice to either awaken or to drift off into a normal, natural sleep. If you are going to awaken, say:

Twenty minutes. Wide awake.

If you are going to drift off into a normal, natural sleep, say:

I am now going to drift off into a normal, natural sleep. When I awaken, I will feel fully rested, calm, and at peace with myself, the world, and those around me.

CHAPTER 5
KEY #2: SELF-TALK
FROM DENIGRATING TO ELEVATING

The more man meditates upon good thoughts, the better will be his
world and the world at large.
—Confucius

el e vate (el *uh* veyt)

ver

1. to move or raise to a higher place or position; lift up.

SELF-TALK IS EXACTLY WHAT it sounds like. It's
your internal dialogue – the words you use when you talk to
yourself either in your own mind or out loud. It's been established
by neuroscientists and psychologists that most people carry on an
ongoing dialogue, or self-talk, of between 150 and 300 words per
minute. Fortunately, most of this self-talk consists of mundane,
routine, and harmless thoughts such as "I'm hungry," or "I need to
get my hair cut soon."

The probability of danger rises, however, when this internal
dialogue takes on a negative connotation such as, "I'll never be as
good as she is," or "I look at food and gain weight." When this kind of
self-talk becomes habitual, you create limiting beliefs about yourself

and about your abilities that may, if left unchecked, go on to become self-fulfilling prophecies.

For those of you who are academic-minded, consider Expectancy Theory (and the Placebo Effect), which states that you don't always get what you want, or what you work for, but you will more often than not get what you expect. If you expect to not make a lot of money, you won't. If you assume you're going to succeed and make a lot of money, you will.

If you think negative self-talk isn't that big of a problem in life, listen to what people say about themselves. I promise you won't need to listen very long before coming across a fellow worker or friend saying something condescending about themselves or something about how fat they are, or how that can't do anything right, etc.... At the same, observe how that person says things like, "I just can't do it!" or "I must be stupid." They don't realize that their language simply reinforces—and often causes—their deficiencies.

There are many self-talk mistakes that people commonly make when they want to let go of excess weight or find their soul mate, or start to eat healthier. Among them are:

- *Focusing on the past or future*
  "I'm terrible at relationships. I always attract bad guys who aren't interested in real, reciprocal relationships." "I can't believe how badly I messed up my life." These are classic examples of not letting go of past mistakes. It's just as counterproductive to worry about what might happen. As a human, you always have control over the present moment, and that's where your thoughts need to be. You are in control of your own thoughts.

- *Focusing on outside factors beyond your control*
  "If I get wet when it rains, I'll get sick." This type of thought is a waste of your mental energy and can only hurt your confidence and your health. Work your hardest to keep your thoughts on controllable factors, and don't assume two things are related when they might not be. And furthermore, don't assume the worst.

- *Focusing on weaknesses during everyday life*
  The time to focus on your weaknesses is when you are evaluating yourself for what you need to change or improve. You can use that information to chart your new course to retrain your brain. However, dwelling on your weaknesses during everyday life only serves to decrease your confidence and make you more nervous and tentative in your ability to reprogram yourself. The ONLY reason to go over the negatives is to use them to create more positive thoughts to replace them with. I have included charts in the Perfect Enough Companion Book to help you identify the negative words and phrases you use, and replace them with positive self-talk.

- *Demanding perfection*
  Anyone who says "I need to be a perfect" is setting themselves up for grave disappointment and poor self-image. The same is true for people who berate themselves for every small mistake they make. Everyone makes mistakes, but it's the admirable people who can make mistakes and continue their lives unfazed. It's great to work towards a balanced everyday life if that's what motivates you, but it's unrealistic to expect to live everyday in a perfect

world. There is no such thing as a perfect world.

Perfection assumes that no matter what you do, there is some other, higher, better level that you're working toward but that, by definition, you'll never achieve. The idea of perfection makes people drive and strive and exhaust themselves, only to constantly feel inadequate and self-critical. Perfection is based on a mistaken notion that a specific state of appearance (or performance or material environment) is the only answer to our deepest intellectual, emotional, and spiritual hungers.

If you want to demand something of yourself, demand that you do your best at each moment, and do everything as correctly as possible.

THE BIGGEST FEARS KEEPING MOST PEOPLE FROM POSITIVE SELF-TALK

Most people have what they think are two positive, useful reasons for NOT speaking positively about themselves:

1. THE FEAR OF BEING SELFISH.

If, like me, you were taught that good people take care of others first, taking care of yourself ends up being interpreted as selfishness and bad. Therefore, your fear of being selfish is somehow alleviated by cultivating negative self-talk.

2. THE FEAR OF BEING THOUGHT OF AS CONCEITED.

If, like me, you were taught that only self-centered, conceited people speak well of themselves, you developed a habit of speaking ill about yourself to avoid being labeled conceited.

CHANGING YOUR SELF-TALK

There are two ways to eliminate negative self-talk. One is through a process commonly referred to as thought-stopping, which involves four steps:

1. Become aware of self-talk.
2. Stop the negative.
3. Replace with positive.
4. Practice the act of stopping negative thoughts.

Sounds easy, doesn't it?

The only problem is that for thought-stopping to be effective, it requires a lot of practice on the conscious level. The way we think about and talk to ourselves can be a difficult habit to break, considering we've been doing it a certain way for our entire lives. To improve your self-talk this way, you need to work hard to learn to recognize when you're engaging in negative self-talk, then you need to work equally hard at stopping those thoughts and replacing them with positive ones. That requires energy, effort, and diligence.

Fortunately, there's an easier, faster way of changing your self-talk, and it requires very little effort because you use your subconscious mind. Your subconscious mind is what tells you that you need to stop at a red light or pedal the bike to make it go. These are actions that, over time, cease to require conscious thought and seem to happen on their own, just like self-talk.

In order to change things that are ruled by the subconscious, there are a couple of things you can do on the conscious level, but the bulk of the transformation will occur (and occur the fastest) if you work with the subconscious through hypnosis.

One of the things you can do on the conscious level is to be vigilant about your vocabulary. I suggest doing some vocabulary building, and while you're at it, some weeding out, as well. There are a handful of words that most people frequently use, which affect the subconscious so negatively that, in my opinion, they should be removed entirely from the human vocabulary. Meanwhile, there are a couple of words we should all be using more often.

WORDS TO AVOID WHEN TALKING TO YOURSELF (OR ANYONE ELSE)

• TRY

Try is one of the most poisonous words in the English language. This venomous little word can cause much misery. To TRY means to test, to attempt to do something. But its connotation is undermining, as it creates three reactions in the subconscious.

1.   It programs failure. If at first you don't succeed, try, try . . . again. The ellipse between "try" and "again" means over and over again. Failure is implicit in the word Try. I tried to lose weight (but failed). I tried to be a good father (but failed). I tried to remember people's names when I meet them (but failed).

2.   Try is a wholly-negative word. Because life requires a total commitment, and because try gives you an ideal way to escape responsibility for doing or not doing something, many people hide behind it. They refuse to commit themselves to yes or no. It's so easy to seek the middle ground and say "I'll try," whether you want to or not. As you utter the word try, your subconscious immediately picks it up and says FAIL. Listen to people who use the word TRY a lot. Invariably, they're failure-oriented and frustrated.

3.   TRY is not an action word. It doesn't give you anything to do. For instance, you hear the word sing, run, or sit, and

your processor gives you something to do with them. Now to that with the word try. What are you doing to do with try? *Replace self-defeating talk with "I'll do my best."*

- ## HOPE

Every word you speak or hear causes a certain kind of emotional and physical response. HOPE transmits a subconscious image, which promotes a feeling of anxiety—the subtle dread that something bad is about to happen. "I hope I get a raise" creates a negative response. There's an unhealthy feeling and serious doubt about what you know or, at the very least, about the outcome. And this emotional part of the equation takes place without your conscious awareness because our emotions are rooted in the subconscious.

- ## PROBLEM

When you use the word PROBLEM you are emphasizing an obstacle and generating a feeling of helplessness; that's why this word is so lethal and every self-help guru will tell you to eliminate it from your vocabulary. If you dwell on difficulties, barriers, or defects, the subjective mind accepts your thinking as a command, and then proceeds to work to produce the same in your external world. Replace problem with something like "challenge."

- ## CAN'T

Cindy, age 8: *Mrs. Richmond, can I go to the bathroom?*
Mrs. Richmond: *I don't know Cindy, can you?*
I remember that same exchange occurring over and over again in grammar school. It was an effective way to remind us kids that "can" means having the physically ability to do something. "Can't," therefore, means that you are physically unable to do something.

That's a very powerful, very negative concept.

When you say "can't" you often mean "won't," which implies you have made a conscious decision to not do something. My suggestion is to say what you mean. If you mean "I choose not to," say so. After all, most people know that when you say "I can't" you really mean "I won't," anyway, and they'll appreciate your honesty.

• NOT

Have you ever told yourself, "I will not eat that chocolate chip cookie, I will not eat that chocolate chip cookie," and then ate it anyway? We've all repeated similar phrases and had the same outcome: disappointment. Why? Because the subconscious is incapable of producing the word "not" in your behavior. Instead, it produces everything but "not." In other words, it produces the behavior that supports "I will eat the chocolate chip cookie." Need more proof? Quick—don't think of a green polar bear sitting next to you. What happened?

Your knowledge of how your subconscious deals with (or doesn't deal with) negative words like "not," "don't," and "won't," will be especially useful when you're constructing affirmations for yourself. But as for your daily language, starting today, always state the outcome you desire in the positive, such as, "I am confident in my ability to lose weight."

• BAD

We all have had experiences that were unpleasant for us. But were they really "bad?" I think using the word "bad" introduces negativity into your life, and negativity attracts negativity. We have visceral reactions to certain words. If you were to say "hate" over and over, how do you think that would make you feel? Likewise, what kind of feeling would you produce by repeating "love" over and over? What do you think happens inside you when you say you've had a "bad" day? Probably not something good. And I bet after you've labeled your day "bad," you expound on all of the "bad" things that happened *to you* that resulted in your "bad" day. And now, you've made yourself into a victim, too.

As for making "bad" decisions, as we all know, some decisions appear to have negative consequences at first, but ultimately pay off in a very positive way. Refrain from judging and labeling things as negative, as doing so just sets you up for further negativity.

• Must/Gotta/Have to

There is very little that we "must" do in order to survive. The list doesn't include grocery shopping on a certain day, buying the latest designer jeans or mowing the lawn before noon. Before you say you "have to do" something, think about it and say what you mean. Maybe you'd "prefer" to do your grocery shopping on Monday mornings, as fewer people shop at that time. Maybe you'd "like" to buy new jeans to keep up with your neighbors. But to use a word like "gotta" is to gravely overstate the importance of the thing you wish to do or have.

What you really mean is that you are making a choice to do something or buy something. And if that's what you mean—say it. When you don't, you hide behind a false notion that you are somehow being compelled or forced to do something—that you're not responsible. Rather than hiding behind a nonexistent taskmaster, admit what you want and don't want. Take ownership of your choices.

• Always/Never/Completely

"I never eat dessert," said the woman eating dessert

and trying to make herself feel better about it.

"You always criticize me," said the husband to his wife.

"I'm completely underappreciated at work," said the woman who still has a job.

Always, never, and completely are definitive words that are rarely accurate. And they have the added problem of angering the person you're speaking with, as most people immediately catch them. When you use these words, you come across as linguistically lazy, and unconcerned with accuracy. In other words, you don't sound credible. Think twice before you utter these words.

CONTROLLING YOUR INTERNAL AND EXTERNAL DIALOGUE

Cancel and *Snap it!* are methods I use to help people stop their negative thinking (i.e., stinkin' thinkin'). You are the only person who can, within a moment of thinking or saying something, stop that thought. You are at the control panel of your thinking. *Cancel* immediately stops your thought, and *Snap It!* provides you with an uncomfortable feeling that you then associate your negative talk. In short order, you will condition yourself to avoid the bad feeling, by way of stopping what creates it (your negative self-talk).

CANCEL

The moment you catch yourself saying something negative, say "cancel," out loud, and replace the thought with something positive. If you have difficulty coming up with a replacement, override your negative thought or word with the image of a purple elephant. *Why?* Because there's no such thing as a purple elephant; it doesn't exist. Therefore, you couldn't have developed any kind of negative association with it. It merely takes up some space for a moment, and you move on. Cancel works well for don't, not, and woulda/coulda/shoulda, as well!

SNAP IT!

In order to reinforce your *Cancel*, you can snap a rubber band on your wrist. I learned this from Bob Reese, author of *Develop the Winner's Mentality*. Snapping the rubber band biologically triggers the canceling of the negative thought; the slight pain changes the thought on a deeper level than the *Cancel* alone. Optimally, you then replace your thought with a positive one. And again, if you have difficulty coming up with one in that moment, envision a purple elephant.

> *"Just as changing your life can change your language,*
> *changing your language can change your life."*
> —Dr. Dan Becker, Director of the Enhancement
> Program at Canyon Ranch

THE TWO MOST POWERFUL WORDS YOU CAN USE

* I AM

These three letters, when put together like this—I am—are a powerful tool for both negative and positive self-talk. *Why?* Because your subconscious will assume the identity of whatever follows them. Consider "I am so fat" and "I am in great shape." If you were to rearrange those sentences, you'd end up with "So fat, I am." "In great shape, I am." It implies that you and the state of being you describe are inextricable. You and "so fat" are the same thing; you are one. So if you're trying to lose weight, you'll have a very difficult time, as you are carrying around with you the very obstacle you seek to eliminate.

TIPS FOR IMPROVING YOUR AUTOSUGGESTIONS (I.E., YOUR LANGUAGE)

Here are some simple rules to follow when structuring your language—to yourself or to others. You can also use these rules when creating affirmations or suggestions when writing your own self-hypnosis script for losing weight, quitting smoking, or whatever else you'd like to accomplish. Remember that your language creates action in the world and that language (both negative and positive) programs your subconscious. And when you're in Alpha state, your language will program your subconscious very quickly, and very easily, so as they say, *"Be careful what you wish for . . . "*

1. **Be realistic.** Though your subconscious mind doesn't recognize the concept of impossible, and will work on anything, there are five areas to avoid, particularly when you are in Alpha state.
    a. *Avoid working on the mind of another.* The one mind you know you can control is your own. Besides, the universe doesn't reward people who try to control the minds of others.
    b. *Avoid attempting to change the orderly progression of time.*
    c. *Avoid thinking you can call upon knowledge, information, and experience you don't have* (e.g., you can't fly, you don't have bionic vision or hearing, and if you have no experience in running, no affirmation or suggestion will make you an instant marathon runner).
    d. *Avoid the attempt to make physical changes that are impossible* (e.g., although some nonhuman animals can

re-grow limbs, we cannot. And although I have heard people tell me they used affirmations to increase their bust size, I'm a bit wary of this technique.)

   e. *Avoid manipulation of that which is beyond your control* (e.g., the weather—even on your wedding day).

2. **Phrase everything in the present time.** When you say, "I will," you're not really committing to do anything now. In fact, you're not really committing to do anything at all; all you're doing is saying you plan to do it . . . later. And for most people, later never comes. Create a strong mental image of your objective "NOW" and let your subconscious produce it for you.

3. **Always use a completely non-resistant (positive) approach.** As long as you talk about what's bothering you, you give it energy; you feed and nurture it simply by paying attention to it. And that makes it more likely that it will live on and recur. Instead, make no mention of what's bothering you. Create a dynamic and positive image of your objective.

4. **State your objective clearly.** Fuzzy, vague goals produce little in the way of results. Always work for the strongest possible response—feelings and pictures. Know exactly what you want, and state it and see it in full color and three dimensions, along with all the feelings it elicits.

5. **Stress activity.** Stress the activity toward your objective. Visualize your active participation. Begin your activity NOW.

6. **Visualize.** Remember that Alpha consciousness responds only to mental images. So when you're in Alpha, imagine the desired goal as you produce Alpha brainwaves. Let the image happen.

7. **Symbolize.** Any concept, goal, or objective that doesn't lend itself easily to visualization can be readily impressed

into the subconscious mind by simply assigning a symbol
to it. For example, whenever anyone says "refrigerator,"
an image appears in your consciousness. You then have a
feeling of delight, a feeling of anger, a blah feeling, a feeling
of excitement—any number of responses are triggered
according to your experiences. In this same manner, you
can deliberately use words, colors, objects, people, things to
trigger entire affirmations and/or suggestions.

Here are some examples of helpful affirmations that my clients
often use:
- I handle stress and tension appropriately and effectively.
- My mood is calm and relaxed.
- I cope well and get on with my life during times of stress.
- My breathing is deep, slow, and calm.
- I am a confident and believe in myself.

It's crucial to your success that you teach yourself to recognize
unfair self-criticism and turn it into empowering self-talk. Practicing
empowering self-talk and working on your mindset is just as important
as practicing the technical aspects of your life.

Some of my clients find it extremely helpful to write little reminders,
goals and affirmations on note cards and place these cards where they
can see them at the start of their day. If you're having trouble with your
mindset, try making a note that says, "I am relaxed and confident that
I am achieving my ideal body weight." Repeat this phrase to yourself
often with a lot of enthusiasm. Before you know it, you'll notice an
improvement and you will lose weight!

It's especially effective to say your affirmation before you go to
sleep and as soon as you awake. You're so close to being in your
subconscious at those times, that you're practically hypnotized. When

you feed your subconscious mind with premises that are true and positive, you will create those true premises in your life.

Please note that this isn't prayer. This is the science of the mind. You are not praying to God to make something happen or to solve some problem in your life. If any kind of prayer is part of this at all, it would take the form of a prayer of gratitude for giving you the gifts that have allowed you to reach this point in your life, where you are poised to make your dreams come true. I am thankful for a brain that functions in such a way that I am able to maximize what I learn and then help others. God provided me with a wonderful tool, which my mentor, Dorothy Gates, taught me how to use. As a result, doors opened for me and I realized the power of my intention. By staying in my own power of intention, I continue to find ways to help others understand their brains the way I have come to understand mine. But all that didn't happen because I prayed to God for it—it happened because I made it happen.

It is necessary to not in any way connect what you are doing to create and re-create your life in a more positive way to your notion of what God and/or your religion has planned for you, if you have such notions. When I discuss enhancing or re-creating your positive self-talk to enhance your life, I'm referring to your ability to use positive self-talk, energy, thought, and the universal laws to your advantage. The fact is that you can choose to create a certain life for yourself. You can choose to be negative and unhappy; if you are negative and unhappy I believe that on some level it's because you have chosen that. Just remember that at any moment, you can choose to be positive and to enjoy life. It's not always easy, but it's always possible.

ACTION STEP

EVALUATING YOUR SELF-TALK

Our self-talk has been cultivated for years and depends on a variety of factors, including our parents, friends, teachers, and life experiences (the "proof" of who we are). Fortunately, no matter what your self-talk is like today, you can change it by replacing any self-defeating words or phrases with elevating ones.

Follow these steps to transform your negative self-talk into positive self-talk:

1. Acknowledge that your self-talk is negative and in need of improvement.
2. Evaluate yourself.
   a. Make a list of words and phrases you often use that you would like to eliminate from your vocabulary.
   b. Make a list of words and phrases you would like to use more often. Notice how rereading the items on this list makes you feel better about yourself. Add items each day and reread the entire list each day.

ACTION STEP

MODELING POSITIVE SELF-TALK

- Who speaks well of themselves and their life and future?
- Close your eyes and imagine that person.
- Envision how the person stands, how they walk, and how they use their hands and eyes. Listen to that person speak.
- Imagine that person interacting with others. What does their voice sound like? What kind of things do they frequently say

to describe their career and relationships? Observe how the other people react to your person who speaks well of their life, yet isn't boastful.

- Imagine yourself standing close to the person you'd like to model. How do you feel? Can you feel their contentment?
- Pretend you're a human sponge and soak up all their good language and feelings.
- Turn to the people in your vision and watch them react to you the same way they reacted to the person you're modeling. Feel the respect and admiration from those around you.
- Now, open your eyes.

ACTION STEP

FILL-IN SECTION #2 OF YOUR *DISCOVER* OUTCOME DEVELOPMENT BOARD

Cut out and paste photos and words that represent your model of Positive Self-Talk as well as your past success onto section #2 of the Outcome Development Board from your Toolkit (#2 is on the top row, second from left, if you're making your own poster). Remember to post it someplace where your conscious and subconscious can continually see it and benefit from it. If you're keeping a notebook, write your feelings and thoughts about your goals for your self-talk. You are creating a story with your board and your notebook of what you want your outcomes to be, so begin your story with "I am . . . " Here are some tips for choosing the most effective images:

- What represents positive talk or words to you?
- Is there a place that you think of that creates positive thoughts for you?

- List positive words that you would like to say and/or think more often.

ACTION STEP

USE HYPNOSIS TO TURBO-CHARGE YOUR NEW SELF-TALK

Everything we've done so far is on the conscious level. Now, let's turbo-charge the improvements you'd like to make regarding your self-talk by enlisting your subconscious through hypnosis. As with any self-hypnosis script, you must relax yourself first by using Instant Alpha Conditioning. You can read the positive self-talk script each time, you can record yourself, or you can listen to the Perfect Enough CD called "Positive Self-Talk." By reprogramming your subconscious mind, you automatically embed positive words and thoughts into the deeper levels of your mind and those words soon become your own positive self-talk.

Let's work with 88% of your brain, and get your every thought to be more positive!

INSTANT ALPHA CONDITIONING

Instructions:

1. Use the word you selected to replace the longer version of the Alpha conditioning technique. Read the following script and let Alpha occur each night, before retiring, for 21 nights. Read aloud, with feeling.

2. Proceed immediately to the script for Positive Self-Talk.

S	M	T	W	Th	F	Sat

From this moment on, each and every time I desire to attain the deep state of total relaxation, I am instantly and fully relaxed, as I am now drifting into the Alpha state of consciousness. The moment I think my chosen word _____, Alpha occurs. This word has an effect only when I use it and only under the proper circumstances. Each and every time I do use it I am fully prepared to receive positive, beneficial and constructive suggestions, impressing each one deeper into my storage and memory facility of my brain.

From this moment on, _____ triggers deep relaxation of my mind and body. I feel Alpha occur. I feel wonderful. I feel comfortable. I am totally receptive and responsive to my own creative ideas and suggestions. I am bathed in a glow of quietness, peace, and serenity. My chosen word works only when I deliberately use it for deep relaxation to attain Alpha consciousness. Its use in regular conversation has no effect on me whatsoever. From this moment on, each and every time I desire the deep state of total relaxation, I am instantly and fully relaxed upon saying _____. Because my subconscious must follow my command, each and every time I desire total relaxation, I am instantly and fully relaxed when I think my chosen word_____ _____. I feel a deep sense of gratification as this word programming becomes a reality. Feeling wonderful, generous, alive, and eager to increase my positive self-talk . . .

POSITIVE SELF-TALK

When negative thoughts enter my mind about myself, I mentally say the word "CANCEL" to myself. I replace any negative thought that I may have with a positive one. Positive thoughts remain within the conscious portion of my mind much longer and much clearer than ever before. Without fail, without exception, without excuse, each and every time a negative thought or idea enters my mind I mentally say the word "CANCEL" to myself. My personal life is in order, my private life is content, and my health is in correct order. I see myself how I want to be. I am positive, happy, healthy and glad to be alive.

I know that being positive, happy, healthy and glad to be alive is called being "balanced." I am balanced. I understand that being "balanced" is when I feel that I am living every day happier. It is an unstoppable, powerful confidence that means that I am the best that I can be. I am always doing and achieving what I set my mind to do. I am thankful that through the power of positive thinking I have the ability to create positive actions. My internal positive self-talk allows me to achieve whatever outcomes I want to work toward. I know that when I practice positive self-talk, my subconscious mind allows positive thoughts to flow through to the conscious mind. It is easy for me to learn and create positive ways to think in all situations. It doesn't matter in the least what has happened in the past, because I am choosing to be positive now and in the future.

Every day in every way I am physically stronger and more fit. I am more alert, more wide-awake, and more energetic. Every day, from the moment I wake up, I remain deeply interested in whatever I am doing. When I work, play, my mind is much less preoccupied with things I cannot change and much more with things I can change and I'm about to change. I focus on my task at hand. Every day I live life with nerves that are stronger and steadier. When I am living life to the fullest, my mind is calm, clear and composed. I think clearly, I concentrate easily, my memory is sharp, and I see things in their true perspective and do not allow them to get out of proportion. Every day that I live my life I am emotionally calm and tranquil. I feel a wonderful sense of personal well-being, personal safety and security.

I am completely relaxed and tranquil. I have confidence in myself and in my ability to enjoy life, living with a positive attitude. I am optimistic, happy and confident. I stick up for myself, I stand on my own feet, and I hold my own ground. Things happen exactly as I wish for them to happen in my everyday life. I remain cheerful and optimistic.

No matter what is going on in my life, I always remain positive and free from negative self-talk. I am confident in my everyday abilities to enjoy life and "CANCEL" out any negative and harmful self-talk that I may have. I easily learn more positive words and statements to replace habits of negative thinking. I remain with a clear outlook for a wonderful and successful future. Every time I see the color red, in or out of my conscious awareness, it reminds me that I am positive and living my life with balance.

This entire suggestion is represented by the letter "I" of my sub-key word "Discover." Anytime I think, say, or see the word "Discover," all suggestions keyed to this word are automatically activated, stimulated and work for my benefit.

You now have the choice to either awaken or to drift off into a normal, natural sleep. If you are going to awaken, say:

Twenty minutes. Wide awake.

If you are going to drift off into a normal, natural sleep, say:

I am now going to drift off into a normal, natural sleep. When I awaken, I will feel fully rested, calm, and at peace with myself, the world, and those around me.

Whatever the mind can conceive, and believe, it can achieve.
Napoleon Hill, *Think and Grow Rich*

CHAPTER 6

KEY #3: PERSISTENCE

FROM HESITATION TO
DETERMINATION

Though he be ever so tired by repeated failure, let him begin his
operations again and again; for fortune greatly favors the man who
perseveres in his undertakings.
—*Hinduism. Laws of Manu 9.300*

per sist ent (per **sis** t*uh* nt)
adjective
1. persisting, esp. in spite of opposition, obstacles, discouragement, etc.; persevering.

OBSTACLES ENTER THE LIVES of all of us, sometimes on a daily basis. But it is how you handle the obstacles that will determine the outcome and how much you will grow and learn from the experience. Many people choose to shy away when an obstacle presents itself rather than moving through it. They have lots of rationalizations for not facing obstacles, but most of them aren't valid. The fact is, we run from obstacles because we are afraid. What kinds of fears keep us from persistence?

- Fear of making mistakes
- Fear of success
- Fear of failure
- Fear of conflict
- Fear of disappointing
- Fear of disappointment
- Fear of change

Persistence is a powerful force in your personality. It is persistence that allows you to fix your attention firmly on a goal and see it to completion. It is persistence that positions you to achieve your goals with ease, confidence, and pleasure. But how do you cultivate persistence?

DON'T BEAT YOURSELF UP

Do you condemn yourself for things that you did in the past? Don't worry, everyone does at some point. Perhaps there are choices you made at crucial turning points in your life that you'd like to take back. Maybe you treated someone you cared for poorly and wish you had another chance. At work, perhaps you made a mistake that cost you a client or some money, you're still angry and frustrated with yourself about it.

If you want to be successful in your life, it's crucial that you release the past and not blame yourself for events that have already transpired and that you cannot change. Ask yourself this question: Has beating yourself up about the past ever helped you or made you feel better? In your relationships, has obsessing over mistakes you made in the past ever made you feel better or make better choices? Beating yourself up is a self-defeating behavior. Fortunately, you can stop it right now.

CHOOSING TO CHANGE

Changing your behavior is more than just making the decision to do it. A perfect example is what most people do with New Year's Resolutions. People always say things like, "I'm going to be a more positive person," or, "I'm going to treat my body better."

What keeps many people from accomplishing these types of goals is simple. What do you do after your trainer at the gym teaches you the proper way to do sit-ups? You practice them, right? And within a couple of weeks, you begin to see a difference and feel different, right? What eludes most people is that changing the way we approach things mentally should be handled in the same way. So if you feel like you beat yourself up over past mistakes and you want to change that behavior, you'll be much more successful if you practice, practice, practice.

The successful person takes this approach: If you have done something in the past that you feel you can and should change, then by all means take action. If you have been unkind to someone, apologize to them. If you failed to fulfill a promise you made, take steps to fulfill that promise. If you haven't yet mastered your yoga postures, devote more time to them. If you smoked a cigarette after having quit for a year, work each day at having a smoke-free day.

The unsuccessful person wallows in regret and self-pity over minor setbacks and inadequacies. Naturally, the unsuccessful person is then unable to move forward. The bottom line is that we ought to learn from past mistakes and make adjustments in future behavior. The strategy of berating yourself for past conduct solves nothing and only serves to lower your self-esteem. You create a vicious cycle where negative experiences and negative feelings are reinforced, which leads to more negative outcomes and more negative feelings.

As I've said before, you aren't going to change one bit of your past.

What's done is done. Learn from your past experiences and move on. You did the best you could, given your awareness and understanding of your options at the time. You are human and it is in our nature to make mistakes. You have nothing to gain from self-condemnation except feelings of misery and inadequacy. You can't control what happened, but you can change the road map in your brain that tells you how to deal with it.

If you have a hard time stopping yourself from dwelling in the past, I suggest that you try to focus on your past successes rather than mistakes. Visualizing and thinking about past successes is an excellent way to build confidence and self-esteem. What you think about is what you become. Therefore, when you concentrate on your successes, you help to create future successes. *What are some of your successes?*

Here's one of many suggestions that I make when my client is completely relaxed and in a highly receptive state of mind:

You are grateful and thankful for every experience of the past, and for everything connected with those experiences. You find it easy to let go of your fears. You forgive yourself for every mistake you have ever made. You are a part of life, as we all are, and we all move, live, and think as we have a right to. Life goes on, and so do you: Growing rich in experience and in the capacity to achieve. You are stronger than anything life can offer.

Early in my career as a hypnotherapist, I noticed a trend in the clients that came to me for help with issues of performance at work. All of them were extremely talented, and most were already very successful in their careers; they seemed like people who should have been incredibly confident in their abilities. Yet they indulged in self-criticism and self-judgment, to the point where they were nearly paralyzed by fear at work. Why were they having trouble with their mindset? Because of the standards they were setting for themselves.

A poor or weak mindset normally is the result of over-critiquing one's abilities to a fault. It's a result of negative self-judgment. When highly-skilled, successful and otherwise self-confident clients came to see me, I realized that the reason they were having so much trouble with their performance was that they were judging themselves not against others or against their true selves, but against the *unrealistic expectation that they had to perform perfectly each and every time.*

The result of this pressure was counter-productive stress and anxiety that produced negative self-talk, and a self-destructive attitude that took away from the quality of their performance, which quickly went downhill. And all of this occurred because they expected perfection from themselves.

Persistence is very different from striving for perfection, as perfection is a state that can never be reached. Take a step back. Realize that you are only human and that people make mistakes. Even the most successful people make mistakes. The important part of making a mistake is learning to forgive yourself for your humanness. You must not let imperfections, large or small, get the best of you.

"Mistakes are essential to progress. The willingness to learn from them is the backbone of any progress. The object is to succeed, not to count your mistakes."
—Tae Yun Kim

Demanding perfection from yourself not only pits you against a false ideal, but it convinces you that other people expect flawlessness, as well. The end result is that you'll feel an extraordinarily unnatural and unhealthy amount of pressure in your life, and you'll be afraid of making a mistake because that mistake will reveal you to be less than perfect. And naturally, your mistakes will then be used as evidence of how flawed you really are.

Mistakes don't reflect on you as a person—
the way you respond to them does.

Joan King, a fellow sports hypnotist and NLP practitioner whose focus is on golf, had this to say in one of her seminars several years ago: "Peak performing athletes rarely put themselves down. They talk to themselves positively about what they are attempting to create. They change past negative messages that come up into positive empowering ones. This is a part of their mental training program." She should know.

HOW TO PERSIST

Earlier in this book I discussed how your mind cannot picture the word "not." For this reason, it isn't useful for me to tell you *not* to strive for perfection. What I can recommend is that you eliminate the word from your vocabulary, and that as far as your actions are concerned, you focus on what you *can* do that is useful: be persistent.

Take time each day to remind yourself of all of the things you're good at, all of the ways you are improving and growing as a person (and mother, daughter, father, son, employer, employee, community member). Remind yourself of all the positive experiences you have had, of all the successes you have achieved. Tell yourself that you are brave, smart, balanced, and confident. Tell yourself that you are proud of your achievements and that you believe in your abilities. And, most important of all, remind yourself that each mistake you've made along the way has been a learning experience that has brought you to where you are today.

When you do something well, tell yourself, out loud, "I did that well." And when you do make a mistake, make sure you look for the things you did well or correctly. Do whatever it is you're doing the best you can do it. Expect you can learn and do as well as anyone by getting rid of everything that blocks you mentally, emotionally, and physically (unchecked mental and emotional issues inevitably manifest as physical problems). Tell yourself that you can overcome any obstacle, and recall all the times you overcame obstacles in the past. Congratulate yourself, and expect similar persistence and success in the present.

CULTIVATING PATIENCE

Part of persistence is cultivating patience, as persistence, by definition, means that the overcoming of difficulties may take some time or a few tries. But nothing can stop you; you persevere and are completely committed to success.

With time, if you work smarter (not harder) and embrace that things change but that you are steadfast in your dedication to your goals, you will achieve them. You must like yourself, believe in yourself, and trust yourself.

Impatience is clearly at cross-purposes with persistence, but there are also other obstacles you need to be aware of . . .

TOP 10 OBSTACLES TO PERSISTENCE

10. IMAGINING FAILURE.

If you visualize yourself smoking again, drinking again, living paycheck-to-paycheck, or in yet another abusive or miserable relationship, guess what's going to happen?

9. ACTING NERVOUS.

When you allow yourself to act nervous, your body language, your movement, and your voice, all tell the world how vulnerable you are. Those around you will hear that message, and many people will react negatively and/or judge you as being insecure or maybe even incompetent. And nothing confirms your feelings of insecurity like the absence of confidence from those around you.

8. STRESSING ABOUT WHAT OTHER PEOPLE THINK OF YOU.

"Everyone knows I've been trying to lose weight and they're all just watching and waiting to see if I'll fail again. If I do, they'll lose all respect for me."

7. MAKING UNREASONABLE DEMANDS.

"If this relationship isn't *the one*, I'm never dating again and I'm joining a convent."

6. WORRYING ABOUT THINGS YOU HAVE NO CONTROL OVER.

"If this guy cheats on me, I don't know how I'll recover from it."

5. LACK OF FOCUS.

Have you ever said to yourself, "No matter how hard I work, I'm always afraid I won't have enough money to retire." As you know, if you're thinking about what might occur in the future, you're definitely not focusing on the present moment.

4. MAKING MISTAKES.

If you want to stop drinking and you keep socializing with people you usually get drunk with, your sobriety won't be coming any time soon.

3. Thinking you're not good enough.

"Maybe I'm not talented enough to land such a fabulous client."

2. Negative self-talk.

"I don't have the willpower to make it through the holiday party without eating at least two pieces of cake." And you'll eat at least two, I promise.

1. Allowing past mistakes to consume your thoughts.

"I always meet great guys then suffocate them until they can't stand me and they leave me." Again, focusing on what you did in the past fuels it and gives it life in the present.

PERSISTENCE AS A HABIT

Ninety-eight percent of what you do is because of habit. You are the kind of person you are because you have formed the habit of being that kind of person. Success is a habit. Failure is also a habit. Repetition forms habits, good ones and bad ones. We are slaves to every habit we cannot break. Make good habits and they will make you. Habits are a subconscious function.

Bad habits are not easy to change without help. But with the use of hypnosis and NLP, changes happen easier than you ever thought possible. All you have to do identify the way you procrastinate, then create a map to be persistent. The process of altering habits involves being conscious about what you're thinking and how you're feeling. It requires concentration on developing new skills to replace the ones you've developed so well that they have become unconscious.

Most people need to have a habit of persistence to complete important projects at work and at home. Many people, whether they realize it or not, could complete their projects in less time if they hadn't *developed the habit of procrastination.*

While working with a client who needed to make a few changes that would move him into the next level of productivity at work, we discovered he really didn't like his boss. We then worked on why he stayed at a job he wasn't comfortable at. He said he stayed because he was making good money, and if he used his creative talents he could go to the next level in the company. To rewire the procrastination habit in his daily routine meant we had to find something he *did* like. *The money!*

We retrained his brain so he would be in "action mode" at work, and we did a few NLP techniques that associated the sight of his boss with deep, calming breaths and motivation to complete whatever task he was working on. Finally, I made sure we found a photo of something he wanted to do, and framed it to put on his desk. Therefore, his subconscious mind would pick up on a pleasure he was desiring, and that pleasure would register in and out of his conscious awareness all day. Soon, he noticed projects getting done quicker and he was noticing that he felt better at work. Over time, he developed a habit of persistence, and didn't even realize it.

ACTION STEP

Modeling Persistence

(As always, make notes about this process if that's what works for you.)
- Who represents persistence to you?
- Close your eyes and imagine that person.
- Envision how the person stands, how they walk, and how they use their hands and eyes.
- Imagine that person at work and in their personal life. What habits do they have that tell you they are persistent?
- Imagine that person interacting with others. What does their voice sound like? What do they look like when they're listening? Observe how the other people react to your persistent person.
- Imagine yourself standing close to your persistent person. How do you feel? Can you feel their persistence?
- Pretend you're a human sponge and soak up the persistence of your model.
- Turn to the people in your vision and watch them react to you the same way they reacted to your persistent person. Feel their respect and admiration, and feel your charisma and confidence. Feel your persistence.
- Now, open your eyes.

ACTION STEP

FILL-IN SECTION #3 OF YOUR *DISCOVER* OUTCOME DEVELOPMENT BOARD

Cut out and paste photos and words that represent your model of Persistence onto section #3 of the Outcome Development Board from your Toolkit (or your poster), and make notes regarding this process if that works for you.

Here are some tips for choosing the most effective images:

- Who represents persistence to you? Is there someone in your field who has overcome adversity and obstacles, yet persisted and achieved the kind of success you'd like to achieve?
- Is there an animal that represents persistence and success to you? Beavers, squirrels, and raccoons are all persistent. They all have a goal in mind and work at it until they reach it, despite setbacks.
- Is there a company or brand that represents persistence to you? Cut out their logo and paste it onto your outcome board.

ACTION STEP

USE HYPNOSIS TO TURBO-CHARGE YOUR NEW PERSISTENCE

As I've said, persistence is a habit. You can work at it on the conscious level by practicing it, but to make certain it "takes," you should turbo-charge your efforts at persistence with self-hypnosis. As with any self-hypnosis script, you must relax yourself first by using Instant Alpha Conditioning. Afterwards, you can read the persistence script each time, you can record yourself reading it, or you can listen to the *Perfect Enough* CD called "Persistence."

Now, let's retrain *your* brain to be more persistent!

Instructions:

1. Read each night, before retiring, for 21 nights. Read aloud, with feeling, and let Alpha occur.
2. Proceed immediately to the script for Persistence.

S	M	T	W	Th	F	Sat

From this moment on, each and every time I desire to attain the deep state of total relaxation, I am instantly and fully relaxed, as I am now drifting into the Alpha state of consciousness. The moment I think my chosen word _____, Alpha occurs. This word has an effect only when I use it and only under the proper circumstances. Each and every time I do use it I am fully prepared to receive positive, beneficial and constructive suggestions, impressing each one deeper into my storage and memory facility of my brain.

From this moment on, _____ triggers deep relaxation of my mind and body. I feel Alpha occur. I feel wonderful. I feel comfortable. I am totally receptive and responsive to my own creative ideas and suggestions. I am bathed in a glow of quietness, peace, and serenity. My chosen word works only when I deliberately use it for deep relaxation to attain Alpha consciousness. Its use in regular conversation has no effect on me whatsoever. From this moment on, each and every time I desire the deep state of total relaxation, I am instantly and fully relaxed upon saying _____. Because my subconscious must follow my command, each and every time I desire total relaxation, I am instantly and fully relaxed when I think my chosen word_____ _____. I feel a deep sense of gratification as this word programming becomes a reality. Feeling wonderful, generous, alive, and eager to increase my persistence . . .

PERSISTENCE

The reason I am reading this session is that I want to let go of all negative habit patterns that keep me from being a persistent individual. I am making a decision to be in control of my life by creating the habit pattern of being persistent. I have decided to become persistent in every thing I do in life. I want to be more organized, and to take be in complete control of following through. That's right! I am going to say a phrase with a lot of energy and excitement. I will repeat the phrase in a very special way, silently to myself so only I can hear it, in the privacy of my own mind. I can hear the excitement as my own reality. Each time I say the phrase, I feel the energy and excitement because I know it is my reality and that is exciting.

> "I am persistent and confident in every thing
> I do in life—now and for the rest of my life."

> "I am persistent and confident in every thing
> I do in life—now and for the rest of my life."

> "I am persistent and confident in every thing
> I do in life—now and for the rest of my life."

> "I am persistent and confident in every thing
> I do in life—now and for the rest of my life."

As I follow the release and clear instructions on this session I allow my subconscious mind to let go of all past habit patterns that are not consistent with being persistent. So now as I see myself at the beach. I am getting a mental image, like watching a movie on my own private theater in the privacy of my own mind. I see the ocean – I see the sand - I can feel a gentle breeze. As I visualize this, I make it as real as possible. I see it all in my imagination. And now very, very vividly, I allow myself to fantasize digging a deep hole in the sand. I dig the hole deeper and deeper. Now the hole is big enough and deep enough. I bury all past negative habit patterns relating to not getting things done, and I throw all cluttering habit patterns in it. Now, as I do this I take each negative thought I have about myself—whether it's about my organizational skills, my lack of anything that is negative I feel about myself, and bury each one. So now as I imagine –I make this real. I perceive every detail of this movie in my mind. I am playing the role. I am playing the part and now as I experience burying each fear in my mind. I am putting all negative thoughts about my abilities to get things done in this hole. I notice I can imagine the smell of the sand and the sea. I feel the breeze, and now I have just allowed this to become my own reality. Now as I imagine throwing the sand over the hole, I close the hole—leaving everything in it that I put in it. I have thrown away all the negativity and the negative self-talk. I have thrown away all the negative-based thoughts. I am now open to new suggestions that I will accept and act upon. I am now open to all the warmth, joy and fulfillment that life has to offer. I feel glad to be alive and enthusiastic about my future. I am now calm and relaxed and a sense of peace permeates my body and mind.

I am filling my powerful subconscious mind with a vital awareness of following through with all projects and plans. From now on, persistence is one of my strong points. It is a definite asset. It is a powerful force in

*my personality. I am always persistent when I have a goal to accomplish.
I achieve all of my outcomes. I follow through to see that all my plans and
goals become reality - for I realize that there are no permanent obstacles.*

*There are only temporary obstacles that I can always ultimately
overcome. I do this by keeping my mind and thoughts fixed firmly on
my outcomes insuring that I constantly move towards them. Whenever I
launch new projects, whenever I make bold new plans, whenever I use my
intuition to set fresh goals and objectives, I always follow through. I am
creating them as outcomes, persistent about everything that I do. I always
follow through. I always follow through. I always follow through. I bring
things to completion. I use my positive thoughts to create the power of my
intention to be persistent.*

*Persistence is a powerful force in my personality. I always follow
through, even in little things. I am a person who brings things to
completion. If there are projects around the house that are undone, I give
them my full attention, thereby insuring their successful fulfillment. If
there are activities in my business that needs some attention, or some
follow through in order to be completed, I do so. I follow through. I see to it
that in all areas of my life, I leave nothing undone. My philosophy is one of
following through and getting the task completed.*

*Following my suggestion helps and guides me to go deeper and more
and more relaxed. I have a powerful force in my personality. I am always
persistent when I have an outcome to accomplish. I achieve these goals
in an assured, calm, relaxed way. This builds a lifetime habit pattern of
success and I find that I follow through in all my activities with ease and
with pleasure. It becomes easy for me, because each time that I do a good
job of following through, it is easier to follow through with future activities.*

I know it's important that I am confident in my ability to accomplish whatever I set my mind to. I am persistent in finishing any task I begin. My confidence builds in my own ability to do anything I put my mind to. I realize that the mighty dynamo within me, my subconscious mind, is constantly working for me.

I am building into my life this most desirable pattern of following through, of persistence, a stick-to-it-iveness and of always getting the task completed. For by doing this, I am taking giant strides towards achieving all my goals of having a powerful personality.

This ensures genuine success and satisfaction in all phases of my life. I find myself enjoying the satisfaction of a well-organized life. I relax completely. I fill my powerful subconscious mind with the awareness of my goals, relaxed and receptive.

I always find a way to figure out what I need to do to get any job done. I am committed to being persistent. Whether I ask others for help or I go within myself for the answer, I always find a solution. I grow stronger every day and with every day that passes. I have wonderful outcomes on every project I plan and implement. I have a very powerful personality. I grow and move forward in life with real purpose, being and becoming the person I intend to be. I am energized and excited about life and everything it has to offer. I use my powerful ability to stay on task and complete projects to succeed at whatever I do.

Through my magnet within I have a powerful force in my personality. My habit pattern in life is to always be persistent when I have a goal to accomplish. I achieve my goals in an assured, calm, relaxed way. This builds a lifetime habit pattern of success and I find that this happens automatically as I become the best me I can be with ease and with

*pleasure. It becomes easy for me because each time I do a good job of
following through, it is easier to follow through with future activities.*

*Every time I read this session I grow more confident and self-assured
in every way. And each time I attempt to achieve this wonderful sense of
relaxation, I find I do it quicker and easier than the previous time. Each time
I do it quicker and quicker. Each time, allowing myself to go much deeper
relaxed, much quicker, and enjoying it more and more. Every time I allow
my body to relax, I feel better. And the better I feel, the more my body relaxes.
With marvelous, wonderful, good feelings going through my body, and happy,
contented thoughts going through my mind. Be still and feel good.*

This entire suggestion is represented by the letter "S" of my sub-key
word "Discover." Anytime I think, say, or see the word "Discover," all
suggestions keyed to this word are automatically activated, stimulated
and work for my benefit.

*You now have the choice to either awaken or to drift off into a normal,
natural sleep. If you are going to awaken, say:*

Twenty minutes. Wide awake.

If you are going to drift off into a normal, natural sleep, say:

I am now going to drift off into a normal, natural sleep. When I
awaken, I will feel fully rested, calm, and at peace with myself, the
world, and those around me.

CHAPTER 7

KEY #4: LIFE AND ALIVENESS
FROM LIFELESSNESS TO VITALITY

Vitality shows in not only the ability to persist
but the ability to start over.
—F. Scott Fitzgerald

vi tal i ty (vahy-**tal**-i-tee)
noun

1. The capacity to live, grow, or develop: plants that lost their vitality when badly pruned.
2. Physical or intellectual vigor; energy.
3. The characteristic, principle, or force that distinguishes living things from nonliving things.
4. Power to survive: *the vitality of an old tradition.*

WHAT'S KEEPING YOU FROM growing and developing into who you are meant to be? From living your life with gusto and savoring every moment? What's keeping you from realizing it's your right to be happy, and then creating that happiness for yourself? Might the answer be that you are afraid of something?

What is your fear?

- Fear of death (because if you fully embrace life, you must accept the inevitability of death)
- Fear of pain (the more you allow yourself to feel, the more pain you'll feel)
- Fear of suffering (ditto)
- Fear of loss of love (ditto)

Do you see the pattern? The more vitality you have—the more alive you feel—the greater the probability that you might experience pain.

CHILDREN TEND TO BE MORE FULL OF LIFE THAN GROWN-UPS

As we grow up, we lose a lot of our aliveness. We lose our innocence. And for some of us, we develop such a fear of living fully that we go through life like automatons. We go to work, we come home, we eat, we do housework, we bathe the children and put them to bed, and we do all of this without actually feeling anything. It's as if we're outside of ourselves watching ourselves go through the motions of our daily routines.

What happened? When did the curious child who asked whatever questions made sense to her at the time, become the reserved adult who silences herself rather than ask a "stupid question?" When did the adventurous child who climbed trees, fell time after time, and climbed them again, all to save her imaginary friend, become the tense adult who plays by the rules and sets only "realistic" expectations? When did the enthusiastic child, equally thrilled each time her father came home from work, become the stoic adult who seems bored by the existence of her husband? Where did all of that zest for even the simplest things go?

I don't like being the bearer of bad news, but regardless of what occurred during your childhood and where you fall in the birth order of your siblings (if you have any), your happiness, at this moment, is a *decision*. No one can "make" you feel incompetent, sad, angry, or ugly. Except you.

As I explained previously, you create your world with the words you use. Therefore, you can create new feelings and states of being with the words you use. In other words, you can choose to be happy (or not). And if you are presently not happy, that is because you have created that unhappiness.

I'm not invalidating the reality of anything that has happened in your life. Perhaps, in the past (meaning, before today), someone did things that hurt you physically, mentally, or emotionally. If it isn't occurring right now, it's in the past. Leave it there.

Now, once it's in the past, why would you waste your time being unhappy about it? Why would you choose to be unhappy about something that is over and done with, and that *you can never change?* Getting angry with reality, past or present, isn't productive.

YOU CONTROL YOUR HAPPINESS

Allowing yourself to feel unhappy about the past is a common way to prevent yourself from feeling happiness in the present. This is particularly true for people who have spent most of their adult lives basking in the negativity of their experiences. They become professional victims and martyrs, and thrive on their own misery and the misery of others. They say their parents "made them" this way. If you are one of those people, I understand that it is threatening to read that your misery is of your own creation, and that you can change it—right now.

Each moment is a reincarnation of sorts. With each moment you can choose what kind of person you'd like to be. You can decide that you'll learn the lessons you've been given in the past, and proceed as a wiser, more balanced individual. That is your right as a spiritual being having a human experience.

As for the people who "made" you this way or that, another waste of time is to wonder if things could have been different. They were what they were, and it's time to move on. And if those same people still behave badly to you, remember that although you cannot control their behavior, you can control your reaction to it. If there is anyone in your life who "makes" you react in a way you don't like, simply make the decision to change the way you react. After all, technically speaking, events are all neutral; things happen. And we, as humans, label those things. We assess them and judge them as "good," "bad," "painful," or "tragic." But those are words that describe a perspective. Change your words, and you'll change your perspective. This may sound like an oversimplification, but if you pause and think before you speak—if you choose your words with intent and focus on choosing only positive words, your happiness will increase. We are taught to activate the negative events and experience in life to find out why we are the way we are. We ponder negative experience after negative experience, in order to decode why things are happening to us as they are now.

But I contend that by constantly reliving what we perceive are negative experiences, we only invite further negative experiences. Then we use those recent negative experiences as proof that the earlier ones really did make us who we are. And so on, and so on. Meanwhile, if we just stopped giving life and energy to the past, we would soon find that indeed it does not have to repeat itself. When I say to think before you speak, that pause not only changes your reactions to the past, but it changes the future as well.

Remember way back in the NLP chapter, I presented the presupposition: If you keep doing what you always do, you'll keep getting what you always got. If the way you are framing your life and its events is causing you unhappiness, change the way you frame your life. You must choose happiness, and decide to make it your way of life.

You can choose happiness by:

- Being confident that it exists for you at every moment.
- Deciding to find a silver lining in every cloud.
- Looking in the mirror each day and saying, "I am happy and deserve happiness."
- Being grateful for your many blessings. Remember to have an *attitude of gratitude.*
- Think of happy things. Once you think thoughts of doom, gloom, failure, and fear, those negative things magically begin to appear in your life. If you think about happy, positive things, happiness will find you.
- Surround yourself with positive, happy people. We all know that misery loves company. Well, it's time for you to become the poster child for: Happiness loves company.
- Take time each day to quiet your mind, and if any thought or image intrudes during your quiet time, replace it with the word "happiness." If you meditate or just use hypnosis, use your private time to be positive.
- Happy people bring out the best in others. Bring out the best in other people whenever you can, and even if you don't want to (*especially* if you don't want to).

CHOOSING PEAK EXPERIENCES

Part of choosing to be happy is choosing to experience life with gusto, and have peak experiences. Whether you're planting orchids or biking through the mountains, you increase your vitality when you honor the gift of life by approaching what you're doing with zest. Celebrate all of the things your wonderful body and mind are capable of, rather taking them for granted.

For example, when you first learned how to ride a bicycle, you probably had a good dose of anxiety. There you were, with your mother watching and your father holding the seat and the handlebars, walking along side you. You knew that your father was going to let go soon and you'd be riding *all by yourself.* If you were like most people, you were thinking of everything you had to do: balance, peddle, steer, sit up straight. Oh, and breathe and keep your eyes open.

That's an awful lot to think about, especially when your entire family is watching you. Your heart pounds, you think and think and think about all of the physical movements you have to keep track of, and you are so nervous and so hyper-aware that you actually recall having to send a signal from your brain to your feet to start peddling.

Now, fast forward one year, and picture yourself whizzing around the neighborhood, doing the slalom around the trees, hopping over curbs and doing wheelies. You're in "the zone." The only thing you're thinking about is beating your own record for speeding down the street. Your feet pedal as fast as they can, but know when to stop for an upcoming jump. Your arms put the handlebars up exactly at the right time, and you effortlessly lift your entire body and your bike a foot in the air to hop a large curb. You aren't conscious of any of this, yet it all happens. Your subconscious mind keeps track of every bodily movement, and allows you to dart around the neighborhood, avoiding danger, until you stop safely back in your driveway. You take that for granted now, but isn't it amazing?

The anxiety you had when you first learned how to ride a bike is gone, because you've done it so many times. But there are some things that, even though you've done them before, you still have anxiety leading up to them and while you're doing them. Public speaking, for instance, causes most people tremendous anxiety, and it's an anxiety that doesn't seem to ever decrease. And because anxiety is always present, they don't get the opportunity to enjoy their public speaking. They can't even imagine that it might be exhilarating to speak before hundreds of people. Trust me, it can.

If you have anxiety about public speaking or test taking, hypnosis is a very effective way to release your anxiety; it's like turning the anxiety switch from "on" to "off." It allows you to accept and activate anchors and so that your brain experiences public speaking in a positive way. It allows you to create a map in your brain that replaces the one that says public speaking is terrifying. Remember, the subconscious mind doesn't know the difference from real and imagined, so you can easily fool it into telling you that you are a wonderful, relaxed speaker. However, there is a lot of work you can do on the conscious level to alleviate some of the physical and mental tension you experience. Here are some tips:

- **BE PREPARED.**

No amount of hypnosis is going to help you if you aren't prepared to do your best. (Though hypnosis can make preparing easier.) This includes practicing under conditions that are similar to what you'll experience during your upcoming performance, and while you are doing so anchoring breathing during your practice (your breath will be your anchor). Eat right, sleep well, exercise, do some deep breathing or meditating. Just as athletes regularly train their body to execute precise skills or maintain a certain pace, they need to regularly train the mind to think precise thoughts and focus on specific things. You can also get a self-hypnosis CD from www.lauraking.net to help train your subconscious mind to be the best public speaker. Remember that I used hypnosis to get where I am and to be able to do what I do.

- ## DON'T EXPECT PERFECTION.

Athletes train their physical skills for years, trying to achieve the perfect performance, but I sure wouldn't want to strive for perfection. As I've discussed previously, perfection assumes that there is always another level, and another level, and another level that you can reach. Just the notion of it is exhausting and debilitating to many people mentally, as they will always strive for it and never reach it.

The key is to maintain confident and positive thoughts before and during whatever it is that used to make you anxious. If you do that, your mind and body will respond well, and you'll enjoy yourself. Even test taking can be enjoyable! If your thoughts are concerned with pressuring yourself to achieve perfection, the stress of that unreasonable expectation will prevent you from enjoying yourself and will also hamper your performance.

- ## IMAGINE PEAK PERFORMANCE.

Imagine yourself giving the optimal performance. Create a complete, rich sensory experience. Imagine what you look like, how you feel, what you smell, and what you hear. The more detailed your image is, the better. Note that imagining peak performance and expecting perfection are *not* the same thing. And of course, remember that your brain doesn't know the difference between your memory of something real and something you have imagined. Imagining does not have the pressure and emotion attached to it that *expectation* has. Expectation can lead to disappointment; imagination cannot.

- **CONTROL YOUR ENVIRONMENT.**

You can't control everything, but you can control who you spend time with and how you react to them. If there is someone in your life who "pushes all of your buttons," either don't spend time with that person, or change the way you react to them and their behavior. (The latter is possible, but takes time. The former is a quicker, easier.) If you cannot completely cut out the person who pushes your buttons, at least limit your exposure to them leading up to important events or performances.

ACTION STEP

MODELING LIFE AND ALIVENESS

(Make notes during this process if you need to.)
- Who represents life and aliveness to you? Who chooses to be happy rather than allow obstacles to alter their mood or outlook?
- Close your eyes and imagine that person.
- Envision how the person stands, how they walk, and how they use their hands and eyes.
- Imagine that person interacting with others. What does their voice sound like? What do they look like when they're listening? Observe how the other people react to your confident person.
- Imagine yourself standing close to your person who has chosen happiness. How do you feel? Can you feel their vitality?
- Pretend you're a human sponge and soak up the happiness and vitality of your model.

- Turn to the people in your vision and watch them react to you the same way they reacted to your happy person. Feel their respect and admiration, and feel your happiness and vitality.
- Now, open your eyes.

ACTION STEP

FILL-IN SECTION #4 OF YOUR *DISCOVER* OUTCOME DEVELOPMENT BOARD

Cut out and paste photos and words that represent your model of Life & Aliveness onto section #4 of the Outcome Development Board from your Toolkit (or your own poster), and make notes if that's what works for you.

Here are some tips for choosing the most effective images:

- Unless you know the intimate details of someone's life, it is difficult to say for certain that they are happy. But you will recognize outer signs of happiness, and certainly outer signs of vitality, when you see them. Choose images that *represent* the feeling you want to have and exude.
- Think back to your modeling exercise and how you have defined the kind of vitality you'd like to have. For some people, vitality means action, while for others it means serenity and stillness. Think about that as you choose your images.
- What does life and aliveness look like to you? If your life is full of life and aliveness, what does it have in it? A vacation home? A special trip? Find those images and paste them onto your board.

ACTION STEP

Use Hypnosis to Turbo-Charge Your New Life and Aliveness

After you've done whatever you can on the conscious level to prepare yourself for living life to the fullest—and enjoying it—you can reinforce your love of life and your confidence on the subconscious level. Let's open you to deeper levels of awareness of life and your role in it, along with knowledge that you are all that you aspire to be. Let's retrain your brain toward life and aliveness! As always, we begin with jetting you into a receptive state by way of Instant Alpha Conditioning. After that, you can either read the life and aliveness script each time, record yourself reading it and listen to it, or listen to the Perfect Enough CD called "Life and Aliveness."

Let's kick start your vitality and your enthusiasm for life by retraining your subconscious mind!

INSTANT ALPHA CONDITIONING

Instructions:

1. Read Instant Alpha each night, before retiring, for 21 nights. Read aloud, with feeling, using the word you chose earlier to replace the longer version of Alpha conditioning.
2. Proceed immediately to the script for Life and Aliveness.

S	M	T	W	Th	F	Sat

From this moment on, each and every time I desire to attain the deep state of total relaxation, I am instantly and fully relaxed, as I am now drifting into the Alpha state of consciousness. The moment I think my chosen word _____, Alpha occurs. This word has an effect only when I use it and only under the proper circumstances. Each and every time I do use it I am fully prepared to receive positive, beneficial and constructive suggestions, impressing each one deeper into my storage and memory facility of my brain.

From this moment on, _____ triggers deep relaxation of my mind and body. I feel Alpha occur. I feel wonderful. I feel comfortable. I am totally receptive and responsive to my own creative ideas and suggestions. I am bathed in a glow of quietness, peace, and serenity. My chosen word works only when I deliberately use it for deep relaxation to attain Alpha consciousness. Its use in regular conversation has no effect on me whatsoever. From this moment on, each and every time I desire the deep state of total relaxation, I am instantly and fully relaxed upon saying _____. Because my subconscious must follow my command, each and every time I desire total relaxation, I am instantly and fully relaxed when I think my chosen word_____. I feel a deep sense of gratification as this word programming becomes a reality. Feeling wonderful, generous, alive, and eager to live . . .

LIFE AND ALIVENESS

I continue to instruct my deeper mind to let go completely. Deeper and deeper and deeper. I am a flexible and enthusiastic human being. Life is an exciting adventure. Each day I become aware, more and more aware of the beauty and goodness of people. I like people.

From the alive and loving part of nature, I am filled with energy and enthusiasm. I make friends easily for my energy of confidence flows out into the world from the serene self within. I am confident and serene. I am glad I am alive. I live the life I want to live. From a firm base of love, and enjoy every moment. A new serenity engulfs my being. As the serenity grows within me, I feel the life's enthusiastic loving and take a new step into even deeper levels of awareness of life yet to be recognized. I am preparing myself now to recognize the deeper levels of awareness, and to feel confident in the capacity that I can know and express deeper levels of knowledge and wisdom.

Hidden within the words I repeat to myself, now is the foundation for growth into higher areas of knowing. My mind intuitively knows the meaning behind the words, and gently allows the growth to take place within me. Allowing my faith to be strong and guide me to live my life with the power of intention toward my purpose. The responsibility of producing and delivering this wisdom out into the world gives me the ability to activate my own power of intention. This power gives me life and aliveness.

My feelings let me know I am alive. I am able to express my feelings. I trust my feelings and act on them. I am able to be me, expressing myself with confidence, feeling and trust. Having aliveness is being aware and being in touch with myself. Being alive, each moment, I am personally empowered.

I am flexible and enthusiastic. Life is an exciting adventure. Each day I become aware of the beauty and goodness of people. I like people and people like me. I am filled with energy and enthusiasm. I make friends easily. I am confident and serene. I appreciate myself. I live the life I want to live, and enjoy each and every moment of it.

*Receiving life's energy from everything around me, the more energized
I receive the more energy I give out. I bring to this moment a new image
of myself that refreshes every thought about myself. I now stand tall and
confident of the power within myself. I see myself superbly fulfilling every
moment of my life, knowing that I am all that I aspire to be.*

*Once again, I know that in my deeper level of awareness, I know the
meaning behind the words and bring to this moment a new image of
myself that refreshes every thought about myself. I now stand mentally
tall, confident of the power within me. I see myself superbly fulfilling every
moment with grace, with wisdom. Knowing that the energy behind the
words is reflected in my growth and in my interaction with life. Within
me is intuitive wisdom. I trust and believe that the laws of the universe
will allow me to live life to the fullest, resulting in a far greater, healthier
me, better than I ever imagined.*

*I now have the flexibility, the strength, the drive, and the confidence to
move forward to assume the responsibility of being the person I am meant
to become, with enthusiasm, with purpose, with gentleness. I feel a wave
of excitement washing over my entire being and I feel a wave of serenity
behind it. I know the satisfaction of growth. A new serenity engulfs me
now and I am confident, certain, and fully at ease. The beacon symbolizes
this growth pattern, a light moving in a circle. The circle of love. A light
brightening the path for others. A light leading the way. I see this beacon
now in my imagination.*

*I now superimpose my love over that light and know that it reflects
out into the world the energy given freely from deep within my love given
unconditionally. The beacon is circling now around and around, and I
move quickly and serenely into deeper levels of consciousness. Deeper than*

ever before. Confident and serene in the knowledge that I am safe, that I can handle the love, the flexibility, the preparation I am now enjoying. For I intuitively know I am preparing myself in ways I have yet to acknowledge, to reveal wisdom's deeper levels. This allows me to be serene. I know security and I feel secure. And when the time is right, I express with confidence, enthusiasm, and love.

I feel the warmth permeating from the beacon as it circles now round, and round and round. Deeper and higher. Deeper and higher. So high, I can see with ease. So easy higher and higher. Serene. Calm. Assurance of even greater strength flowing into my awareness. Strength to be, strength to share, strength and wisdom. Wisdom and strength reflected in the energy in which I am now a part. Slowly and with supreme confidence bring back with me what I can. And know that the rest is at this space. Whenever I visualize a beacon in my mind's eye, this space is accessible to me to feel like life's energy is flowing through me. I visualize the beacon and this space is accessible to me. Preparing me in ways beyond my current knowing to accept and then I give out with love and compassion all that I am learning. With an attitude of gratitude about what I want, I am able to allow the power of my intention to become more apparent.

All that I am experiencing is from the love center within my being. Growth and serenity. Growth and strength. Growth and wisdom. Each time I visualize the beacon, circling the light moving in a circle. The circle of love. A light brightening the path for others. A light leading the way. I am that light. I am that light. I am that light.

This entire suggestion is represented by the letter "C" of my sub-key word "Discover." Anytime I think, say, or see the word "Discover," all suggestions keyed to this word are automatically activated, stimulated and work for my benefit.

You now have the choice to either awaken or to drift off into a normal, natural sleep. If you are going to awaken, say:

Twenty minutes. Wide awake.

If you are going to drift off into a normal, natural sleep, say:

I am now going to drift off into a normal, natural sleep. When I awaken, I will feel fully rested, calm, and at peace with myself, the world, and those around me.

CHAPTER 8

KEY #5: HEALTH

FROM ILLNESS TO WELLNESS

Every patient carries her or his own doctor inside.
—Albert Schweitzer (1875-1965)

health ('helth)

noun

1: the condition of an organism or one of its parts in which it
performs its vital functions normally or properly : the state of
being sound in body or mind: freedom from physical disease
and pain —compare to *disease*.

NOTICE THAT LAST PART: health is compared to disease.
Health is the absence of disease. Disease is the absence of
health.

If you are the sum total of all of your thoughts, and you are not in
good health, what does that tell you about your thoughts? They, too,
probably are not in good health. In other words, the language you use
each day, and the thoughts you think at each moment, are probably
in a state of disease.

How would you, on the average day, describe your health? If you wouldn't say, "stellar," "fantastic," or "marvelous," there's something keeping you from being healthy. Yes, there is a genetic component to health, disease, and longevity, but my experience tells me that even the most depressing genetic scenarios can be overcome by people who are positive, loving, and don't view themselves as victims. Likewise, my experience tells me that depressing genetic scenarios can also lead to fear, disease, misery, and untimely death. Here are some of the fears I find most prevalent in clients who have health challenges:

- Fear of aging.
- Fear of death.
- Fear of physical pain.
- Fear of suffering.
- Fear of living life.

Each of us has within us the life-giving, healing properties of the sun's light. Each of us shines with the light that can pierce past experiences and conditions, annihilating them. Each of our bodies is charged with vitality, energy, and health. If you accept the cleansing, healing properties of your body, you will attract the creative power to produce health in your body.

The average child is born healthy, and depending on what he or she is surrounded with (and filled with) the child can either remain in a normal state of health, or deteriorate into an abnormal state of illness. It follows, then, that if the child has developed a state of disease, it can be remedied by surrounding the child (and filling the child) with things, thoughts, foods, and energy that is life-affirming and healing. Healing simply involves the increased inflow of positive, vital forces throughout the body and mind.

The best news about the healing of your body is that it can happen all by itself, if you don't get in its way. *Why?* Because the subconscious mind is the keeper of your body and is on the job all day long, every day of the year. Therefore, if you are experiencing a challenge to your good health, you can order your subconscious to get on the case and resolve the issue each night before you go to sleep. You can give your subconscious a new blueprint for what you want your health to look like, and it will have no choice but to obey you. Remember, the subconscious mind cannot differentiate between what's real and what's imaginary. If you present it with a visual of your healthy, vital self, that is what it will produce.

When I refer to health, I include a healthy weight. Therefore, if you are someone who needs to lose weight, or has battled with your weight for a long time, I am here to say that the solution to your problem may be more in your thoughts than your eating habits.

THE IMPACT OF STRESS

Stress is a major component in most of our lives, and can become a persistent, negative factor that leads to disease. *How?* The more stress you experience, the more you tend to focus on it. You attend to it and give it life and energy and language. You say, "I'm so stressed out," "Life is very stressful for me right now," and/or "I'm under a lot of stress." And once you do that, you tell your subconscious what to produce in your life: more stress. And when your stress level increases, your immunity decreases and you become more susceptible to germs, viruses, and disease. Stress leads to disease. Sometimes it's in the form of a headache, sometimes it's more serious and takes the form of an ulcer, and sometimes the result is cancer.

GENETICS CANNOT BE NEGLECTED

Some of us are genetically predisposed to certain health challenges. Diabetes, heart disease, weight problems, allergies, and asthma are common challenges that have a genetic basis. However, genetics doesn't guarantee anything. The worst thing to happen to many people's health is that a doctor takes their history and tells them the illnesses and diseases and malfunctions that they might experience based on that information. Guess what happens next? They develop those illnesses, diseases, and malfunctions. It's no surprise. Suggestion, accompanied by the supporting evidence of a family history, is a powerful way to convince someone that they might be unhealthy.

HOW TO PRODUCE HEALTH

There are things you can do, on the conscious level, to improve your health. Some of them are:

- Practice relaxation as a method of stress reduction.
- Exercise as a method of stress reduction.
- Visualize positive images about your health. If there are any areas of your body that are currently not healthy, visualize them as healed. In fact, visualize them *healing* themselves.
- Visualize general healing by imagining yourself as surrounded by white, shining light, like that of the healing Sun. Feel the warmth of the light circulate throughout your body and over your skin. Feel the healing as it occurs.

The subconscious mind would probably flawlessly take care of your body and your vitality if you let it, but unfortunately it is never alone. Your conscious mind is always lurking about, planting seeds of doubt and criticism and fear. "The condition of sickness simply means you are going against the stream of life and thinking negatively" (Murphy

2001, 99). When you entertain thoughts that are negative, they soon cling to you and harass you, until they inevitably bring about disease. Eliminate destructive thoughts; they only tear down your body and make it susceptible to any illnesses around you.

YOU MAY BE MORE RESPONSIBLE FOR YOUR HEALTH THAN YOU THINK

If you aren't as healthy as you'd like to be, you may very well be able to control some, or even all of your condition. I'm a firm believer that your health, which includes your weight, is a symptom of something much deeper, and that something is usually a fear and/or the inability to forgive—and that includes forgiving yourself. Whatever you think your health issue is, that aspect of you is merely a manifestation of something else. And that something else is what I want to locate and fix. Once it's fixed, health is restored, and weight is managed.

FORGIVENESS AND HEALTH

Is there someone you need to forgive in your life? Maybe there are a couple of people, and maybe you're one of them. Maybe you've never forgiven yourself for being "a disappointment" to yourself (or someone else) or for making "stupid mistakes." As long as you find it difficult to love and forgive, you will continue to have health problems, including weight problems.

Every single client I have had that has a health problem, does not fully love and accept him or herself. This is without exception. They all think they're not thin enough, smart enough, successful enough, attractive enough . . . they're just not good enough.

What is the basis for the feeling of not being good enough?

Very simply, when you're judging yourself and concluding that you aren't good enough, at that moment, you're living in the past. You're focusing on one moment or series of moments from your past—whether it all happened yesterday or it's been building for your entire life—and allowing that to rule your thoughts. And as you now know, your thoughts rule your life. Therefore, when you judge yourself and condemn yourself for . . . whatever . . . you're allowing your past to rule your life. My favorite quote about this is by Louise Hay, from *You Can Heal Your Life* (1999): "Would you really dig into yesterday's garbage to make tonight's meal? Do you dig into old mental garbage cans to create tomorrow's experiences?" (42).

It makes no difference whether you've created your dis-ease because your parents convinced you that you weren't worthy, or because you blame yourself for not getting the love you deserved. If you're health is compromised, you can begin with this moment to turn that situation around and actually create health, one thought at a time.

Quick. Stop. Right now. Answer this question: What do you think about your weight and health at this moment?

If you used any negative, insulting language, make a commitment to make it the last time you'll use such language about yourself. In fact, you won't even think such things. After all, thinking it is as bad as saying it.

Decide, right now, to cease being angry, frustrated, or hopeless. Decide, right now, to stop blaming anyone for your weight and/or health—and that includes yourself. Decide, right now, that love and acceptance are your only path to healing and sustainable health.

If you aren't willing to change—and to do the work required to change—you may as well close this book, go to your nearest fast-food chain, and get yourself a super-sized order of french fries. And on your way home, get yourself some bonbons or donuts, and call it a day.

If you are willing to do the work, here's what it entails:

- Examining the language you use in our head, and outside of it, to the world.
- Examining your behavior patterns to determine which ones are enabling you to be complacent, and which ones are positive and challenging and will lead to wellness.
- Creating new language that will support your desire for healing and longevity.
- Creating new behavior patterns that will support your desire for healing and longevity.

For some people, this is the first time someone has associated their thoughts, language, and behavior, with their health. If you're one of those people, it doesn't matter that you're late to the party. All that matters is that you're here, and you now have the awareness that what you think, say, and do, dictates what you attract.

Do you mean to tell me that if I'm ill I've attracted my illness?

Yes, but it's not all bad news. I realize that many people aren't willing to believe that they've attracted illness. Illness can be a magnificent and powerful teacher, and perhaps it is not illness you attracted, per se, but the opportunity to learn the lessons you need to learn. Perhaps illness is merely a vehicle for personal growth.

I believe we all have far greater responsibility for our own health than we'd like to think. It's easy to believe that illness is something we have no control over; that it *happens to us*. But the truth is that *we invite it* by cultivating an internal environment that is negative, insecure, and, well, *unhealthy*. Remember, the Law of Attraction says that we get back what we put out. Therefore, if your thoughts and your energy are negative, you will attract other negative energies, including those that can result in disease. And if your internal environment isn't strong and secure, you are likely to succumb to the disease. Like attracts like.

THE FIRST STEP TO ATTRACTING WELLNESS

Your thoughts and your energy need to project wellness, but before they can do that, you need to release the need for illness. You need to let go of your attachment to illness and whatever benefit it gives you. All you want to do is learn what you need to learn and move on.

What's all this about benefits of being ill?
Do I think you consciously desire to be ill to get whatever benefit you get? No. But if you aren't well, that mere fact is my evidence that you have a need to not be well. Do I think you get something positive from it? No. But you get *something* from it. Maybe that something is attention. Maybe that something is an alibi; you get to procrastinate about whatever you really need to do and use your illness as an excuse. Maybe you get to punish a family member who must care for you. Maybe you get to punish yourself for not being who you thought you'd be or for not forgiving someone who hurt you in the past. Or maybe you just plain don't want to move forward in your life. There are myriad reasons you might benefit from being ill, and only you can determine what they are. Again, illness is a teacher. *What's your lesson?*

Letting go is a simple exercise, but like anything else, when it's done on the conscious level, it can easily be fleeting if you haven't already developed a habit pattern of letting go (in the subconscious). And also like anything else, you have to have the desire to make the change. Just as I can't make a smoker quit if he doesn't want to, I can't make you let go of your need for illness if, in your mind, the benefits of being ill outweigh any possible benefits from being well.

THE RECIPE FOR WELLNESS

Positive, affirming thoughts and speech are definitely necessary to create an environment of wellness. However, they can't do it alone; they are part of a recipe where all the ingredients are vital.

What are the other ingredients?

Good nutrition, exercise, interruption-free sleep, meaningful work (whether or not you get paid), and intentional, wakeful relaxation of the body and mind (such as through meditation or prayer) are all components of the optimal environment for health and balance.

Good nutrition means: A way of eating that nourishes the body and allows it to heal itself. In other words, don't get in its way by pumping it with toxins. If you fill your body with junk, it will expend a lot of energy trying to cleanse itself of that junk and return to balance. Meanwhile, if you don't fill it with junk, it has energy for healing and balance. The better you eat, the faster you heal and the better you feel.

What is eating well?

That depends on whom you ask. I'm not a nutritionist, and even if I were, I wouldn't be able to provide a universal diet to all readers. Some people eat a plant-based, raw food diet and swear by it, and others swear by a low carbohydrate, high protein diet. Consult a nutritionist or holistic practitioner for the eating plan that is right for you. And remember that traditional, Western doctors are trained to treat disease with drugs and surgery. Most aren't educated about the healing properties of food and herbs.

What's all the hoopla about meditation?

Meditation is simply relaxation, and though your body is relaxed and still, it's your mind that's the real target. We all have hundreds of thousands of words, ideas, and images running through our minds all day, and if you're like me, you have a difficult time quieting your mind. My thoughts race so much that they often give me a headache. But when I meditate regularly, even for ten minutes a couple of times each day, I get a much needed respite from the madness my mind is capable of producing. It's like a mini-vacation where I close my eyes and clear out every sound and sight from my consciousness and just . . . be.

The more you meditate, the more in touch you become with your body and the signals it's sending you. When you sit down to begin, you can focus on the tips of your toes, all the way up to the top of your head, and feel what each body part is feeling. Feel it against the floor. Feel the texture the skin is resting on. Feel the warm blood flowing. If you experience any moments of discomfort, simply breathe through them and visualize your breath cleansing whatever body part is uncomfortable.

Once you get accustomed to this practice, you'll notice that each body part has its own unique feeling. And when it is not at ease—or worse—you'll immediately know after awhile.

The way a lot of people have learned meditation is by relaxation, combined with guided imagery. However, once you are adding any type of suggestion—either visual or auditory, you are changing the state of conscious awareness. In other words, any time you close your eyes and are being guided deeper and deeper, you are being hypnotized.

I believe that hypnosis gives you the same benefits as meditation. By listening everyday to a relaxation session or by doing the self-hypnosis sessions in this book, you are allowing your mind to go to the Theta and Delta levels, where the mind is allowed to heal the body and the mind is allowed to rest for a moment.

MY BOUTS WITH ILLNESS

Fifteen years ago, I was in pursuit of the perfect body. I had recently had a C-section to birth my premature son, Edward. He weighed just over two pounds and was about the size of my hand. Using an electric pump to supply him with breast milk every two hours for four months, profoundly affected the look and feel of my breasts. And then there was the extra fat I had accumulated after both of my children. I have a plastic surgeon in the family, so that seemed like the right way to deal with my extra fat and disfigured breasts.

The tummy tuck and breast augmentation were a success, but the results were not easy to live with. The doctor chose to give me breasts about three sizes too large! Some women would have loved it, but I didn't; my new breasts kept getting in the way. When I attempted to ride my horse, it was difficult to get in and out of the saddle. And then, of course, there were the men who started conversations with my chest rather than my face. Unfortunately, because I didn't change my eating habits, I started gaining the weight back (which is what happens when someone loses weight but doesn't change their habit pattern of eating).

What happened next changed my life: one of the implants broke. I became very ill, with no energy and brown spots all over my body. An MRI showed the problems and I was diagnosed with fibromyalgia and an autoimmune disease, so I decided to have the implants removed. The doctor did a wonderful job without implants, but my recovery was long and difficult. My doctors had me on at least a dozen medications—something for everything that was wrong. And then there were the sleeping pills and the painkillers.

Then Dorothy reminded me to listen to her tapes, and her Health tape eventually helped me sleep without sleeping pills; I allowed my mind to go to the Theta level for rest and healing. And then I focused on her Pain Management tape, and I was able to get through the day without painkillers. From a medical standpoint, I had a remarkable recovery once I started using Dorothy's tapes and allowing my mind to heal my body. And you can too.

ACTION STEP

MODELING HEALTH

(Record your thoughts and feelings if that helps.)
- Who is a model of health for you?
- Close your eyes and imagine that person.
- Envision how the person stands, how they walk, and how they use their hands and eyes. Imagine how great they look in their clothes. Imagine the bright whites of their eyes and their clear, dewy skin.
- Imagine the daily habits of your healthy person: what they eat, how they sleep, and how they exercise. Step into the body of your healthy person while they're doing healthy things. How do you feel?
- Imagine that person interacting with others. What does their voice sound like?
- Imagine yourself standing close to your healthy person. How do you feel? Can you feel their health and vitality?
- Pretend you're a human sponge and soak up the health of your model.
- Turn to the people in your vision and watch them react to you the same way they reacted to your healthy, fit person. Feel their respect and admiration, and feel your good health. Notice how your body feels alive.

Now, open your eyes.

ACTION STEP

FILL-IN SECTION #5 OF YOUR *DISCOVER* OUTCOME DEVELOPMENT BOARD

Cut out and paste photos and words that represent your model of Health onto section #5 of the Outcome Development Board from your Toolkit (of your own poster), and make notes about your process if that helps you.

Here are some tips for choosing the most effective images:

- Look for images of the body you would like to have, but keep it realistic for your height and body type.
- Be careful of choosing people who look either way too thin, or way too muscular, if you're not willing to put in the time necessary to get that muscular.
- Choose someone doing activities you want to do.

ACTION STEP

USE HYPNOSIS TO TURBO-CHARGE YOUR HEALTH

After you've done what you can on the conscious level, you can program your subconscious to help you attain and maintain good health. Using hypnosis, you can turbo-charge your subconscious to promote a healthier you. As always, you must relax by using Instant Alpha Conditioning prior to reading the self-hypnosis script or listening to your recorded version. A simple way to achieve this step is to listen to the Perfect Enough CD called "Health".

Let's tap into your deeper mind to access your self-healing abilities!

INSTANT ALPHA CONDITIONING

Instructions:

1. Read each night, before retiring, for 21 nights. Read aloud, with feeling. Use the word you selected to replace the longer version of the Alpha conditioning technique. Read the following script and let Alpha occur.

2. Proceed immediately to the script for Health.

S	M	T	W	Th	F	Sat

From this moment on, each and every time I desire to attain the deep state of total relaxation, I am instantly and fully relaxed, as I am now drifting into the Alpha state of consciousness. The moment I think my chosen word _____, Alpha occurs. This word has an effect only when I use it and only under the proper circumstances. Each and every time I do use it I am fully prepared to receive positive, beneficial and constructive suggestions, impressing each one deeper into my storage and memory facility of my brain.

From this moment on, _____ triggers deep relaxation of my mind and body. I feel Alpha occur. I feel wonderful. I feel comfortable. I am totally receptive and responsive to my own creative ideas and suggestions. I am bathed in a glow of quietness, peace, and serenity. My chosen word works only when I deliberately use it for deep relaxation to attain Alpha consciousness. Its use in regular conversation has no effect on me whatsoever. From this moment on, each and every time I desire the deep state of total relaxation, I am instantly and fully relaxed upon saying _____. Because my subconscious must follow my command, each and every time I desire total relaxation, I am instantly and fully relaxed when I think my chosen word_____. I feel a deep sense of gratification as this word programming becomes a reality. Feeling wonderful, generous, alive, and eager to live a healthy life . . .

HEALTH

The reason I am reading this session is because I want to improve my health. I have made a decision to be in control of my life. I have decided to enjoy radiant health. That's right! Great, now I am going to do an exercise that I believe I will really enjoy. In a moment I am going to say a phrase to myself and then I will repeat that phrase with a lot of energy and excitement. I will repeat the phrase in a very special way, silently to myself so only I, in the privacy of my own mind, can hear the excitement as my reality. Each time I say the phrase, I repeat it with more energy and excitement because I know it is my reality and that is exciting. After I say the phrase a few times I will find I believe it and own it to be true for myself.

I am strong, balanced and healthy now and for the rest of my life.
I am strong, balanced and healthy now and for the rest of my life.
I am strong, balanced and healthy now and for the rest of my life.
I am strong, balanced and healthy now and for the rest of my life.
I am strong, balanced and healthy now and for the rest of my life.
I am strong, balanced and healthy now and for the rest of my life.
I am strong, balanced and healthy now and for the rest of my life.

In my imagination, I see myself going across a field to a meadow. I allow my mind to visualize, see or imagine a meadow. I look at all the details. I imagine a gentle breeze blowing. I see the waves as they flow over the grass. I feel the gentle breeze flow through my hair. Breathing in and out and relaxing even more. Deeply and completely as I enjoy this walk. The path that I am following is by a stream. I listen to the sounds of nature. Listen to the bubbling water. Listen to the rustling leaves. I put my hand into the water and notice the crisp coolness. I continue to walk on.

There is a mountain a short distance from me. As I approach the mountain I know deep within that it is easy for me to climb it. Step by step, I climb the mountain. A feeling of complete comfort flows over my body and relaxation allows me to feel comfortable, safe and secure.

I face the sun as it rises like a ball of fire in the heavens. The sun is a source of energy and life. It is the source of expanding rays. I let the sun's rays bathe my body. I let its radiance penetrate deeply into my being. I feel life-giving, healing properties flowing through my body. The sun's tremendous energies flow throughout my entire being, invigorating and strengthening every particle. It doesn't matter in the least what I have experienced in the past. Radiant health is mine right now. I feel it pulsing through me with every breath I take. Every gland, every organ, every tissue in my body is now being charged with radiant vitality, with energy. The power of my subconscious mind keeps my lungs breathing, my heart beating, my blood circulating and every gland and organ operating completely. I know it. I trust it. I believe it. I thank it for serving me so intelligently and so efficiently. At this moment, every part of my body is being cleansed, purified, revitalized.

I am strong, I am well, and I am balanced. I know that there is nothing impossible for my creative mind. Its healing power strengthens and perfects my body right now. I accept it and relax completely. I allow this energy to operate fully and freely. I let my body and mind completely relax. Life circulates normally and naturally through every tissue of my body. Every cell is alive and tingling with dynamic health.

I am building new cells to replace damaged ones. Making rough ones smooth. Every cell is alive and tingling with dynamic health.

Abundant life now operates through my eyes. I can see the beauty of life without effort. My vision is excellent. I see clearly. I hear easily. My hearing is keen and clear. Every gland and organ of my body functions in harmony. I love my body. I have faith in it. I trust it. Every part of it. I think only good thoughts about my body. I relax and handle every situation that life has to offer. I attract to me that is good for my health.

Every fiber, every tissue, every organ, every gland, every part of my body will triple in relaxation when I close my eyes. I feel great, I feel wonderful, I feel fine, with marvelous feelings going through my body and very happy, content thoughts going through my mind. Once my eyes are closed I keep relaxing with every breath I breathe. I give in to the relaxation easily and automatically, and will let myself go, relaxing more and more every time I read this session. I let myself go and all tension leaves my body. All discomfort leaves my body. All of my organs function normally, and all of my glands function normally.

I speak with love and with understanding in a completely relaxed way. I do whatever I should do. Whatever I need to do easily and confidently. I am always conscious of the creative power expressing through me. I allow the feeling of relaxation to flow through my body quietly and peacefully knowing that this creative power with its abundant goodness continuously operates through my thoughts. Through my body and out into my world. I am confident, I am relaxed, and I am at peace. My body is being renewed and strengthened as I relax and allow the sun's rays to bathe my body. I let its radiance penetrate deeply into my being.

I allow the feeling of life-giving, healing properties to descend into my body. It's easy for me to believe in the new positive thoughts about life that I am now incorporating into my everyday thoughts. I let these feelings remain with me. And with every breath I take I continue to relax deeper, deeper, deeper.

As I count from **FIVE** down to **ONE** each one of the suggestions make positive changes through my own thoughts to let my body do what is necessary to be healthy. Allow the feeling of a cool breeze to flow across my skin. Allow the bright sunlight to heal.

FIVE.... Radiant health is pulsing through me with every breath that I take. **FOUR**... Every gland every organ and every tissue of my body is now being charged with radiant vitality and energy.

Number **THREE**... Every gland and organ is operating in harmony. Every part of me is being cleansed, purified, revitalized.

Number **TWO**... There is nothing impossible for my creative mind. This healing power strengthens and perfects my body right now. I accept it. I allow this energy to operate fully and freely. Life is circulating normally and naturally through every tissue of my body. Every cell is alive and tingling with dynamic health. Whatever my mind can conceive my mind can achieve.

ONE... I accept I can love my body. I allow myself to have faith in it. I trust every part of it. I speak with love and with understanding in a completely relaxed way. Easily and competently, and always conscious of creative power expressing through me. Once I close my eyes I will relax quietly and peacefully, knowing that this creative power with its abundant goodness continuously operates through my thoughts, through my body, and out into my world. I am confident, I am at peace.

Once I close my eyes all sounds will fade and all I notice is the sound of the brook. The bubbling water as it winds its way down the mountain. I will begin my descent down from the mountain along the brook, returning to the meadow. And as I return, I find myself eager to sit under a tree. As I sit under the tree, I know that it doesn't matter in the least what I have experienced in the past. Radiant health is mine right now. I feel it pulsing through me with every breath that I inhale. Every gland, every organ, every tissue of my body is now being charged with radiant vitality with energy.

The power of my subconscious mind keeps every gland and organ operating in harmony. My body is finding the balanced place it knows. I know it. I trust it. I thank it for serving me so intelligently and so efficiently. I also realize that at this very moment every part of me is being cleansed, purified by the light. I know that there is nothing impossible for my subconscious mind. Its healing power strengthens and perfects my body right now. I accept it and relax completely. I let this energy operate fully and freely. As I relax deeper and deeper, life's circulates normally and naturally through every tissue of my body. Every cell is alive.

I am allowing the building of new cells to replace damaged ones, making rough ones smooth. Every cell is alive and tingling with dynamic health. I am grateful for my health. Abundant life now operates through me. I love my body. I trust every part of it. I do whatever is necessary easily and confidently. I allow my creative subconscious mind to express through me, knowing that this creative power with its abundant goodness continuously operates through my thoughts, through my body, and through my mind. I am at peace.

As I sit or lie here more comfortable with each second, more relaxed, I imagine in my mind the color blue. For me, blue represents health. Every time I see or even think of the color blue I feel healthy. Blue makes me feel great about myself. The blue of the sky, a blue stripe on a shirt, or even a mental image of the color blue. Blue in any form, real or imagined, is my key to dynamic health. Any time I see the color blue, in and out of my conscious awareness, it automatically doubles this entire session for health in my subconscious mind.

My body is balanced, renewed and strengthened.

Every time I read this session I automatically go deeper relaxed and I automatically double this session in my subconscious mind.

This entire suggestion is represented by the letter "O" of my sub-key word "Discover." Anytime I think, say, or see the word "Discover," all suggestions keyed to this word are automatically activated, stimulated and work for my benefit.

You now have the choice to either awaken or to drift off into a normal, natural sleep. If you are going to awaken, say:

Twenty minutes. Wide awake.

If you are going to drift off into a normal, natural sleep, say:

I am now going to drift off into a normal, natural sleep. When I awaken, I will feel fully rested, calm, and at peace with myself, the world, and those around me.

CHAPTER 9
KEY #6: LOVE
FROM WORTHLESS TO VALUABLE

To love is to know Me,
My innermost nature,
The truth that I am.
—Hinduism. Bhagavad Gita 18.55

Love (luhv)

noun

1. a profoundly tender, passionate affection for another person.
2. a feeling of warm personal attachment or deep affection, as for a parent, child, or friend.

THERE ARE MANY FEARS that may prevent you from loving yourself and others. Among them are:

- The fear of losing the people you love through death or estrangement
- The fear of being considered worthless
- The fear that you're inherently not lovable
- The fear of losing love if you get it
- The fear of the pain that inevitably comes with loving and

195

being loved
- The fear that others will disappoint you
- The fear you will disappoint/not be enough

This chapter will help you reach the realization that you are worthy of love. And when you have embraced that truth, you will be able to love others. As you accept and love others, you are free to live your life with enthusiasm, confidence, and joy.

ATTRACTING LOVE

The best way to attract love, or anything else for that matter, is to be that thing. Be love, and according to the Law of Attraction, you will attract love. As I tell my clients, "Be the person you want to marry," and you'll attract someone just like you.

Any of the fears listed at the beginning of this chapter can get in your way of attracting and accepting love, as fear is the absence of love. But if you exhibit patience, tolerance, understanding, compassion and respect for others, those traits will boomerang back to you in the form of reciprocal, healthy relationships.

An important aspect of love is that it should be unconditional, and as adults we have a difficult enough time loving ourselves unconditionally, let alone anyone else. It's frustrating for us to think of unconditional love when we all make so many mistakes. But mistakes shouldn't be part of the equation. Unconditional means unconditional: mistakes and all.

As for the actual behaviors that all add up to the notion of love, I suggest you make a list of all of the parts of your various relationships that make you happy. Since we're all human and have the same basic wants and needs, odds are what makes you feel loved is what makes others feel loved, as well. Once you've made your list, your next step is to develop the behaviors that exemplify the items. For instance, I notice that people feel loved when others listen to them and carefully consider their thoughts and feelings. People who feel loved are not dismissed by others. Likewise, people who love do not dismiss the thoughts and feelings of others. Therefore, if I want to attract love, one of the things I'll have to do is listen carefully to what others have to say, and take the time and energy to consider—to attend to— their thoughts and feelings.

WHY YOU SHOULDN'T NEED LOVE

Whenever you want to attract something into your life, the worst way to do it is to focus on how much you need it. That's a surefire way to never getting it. I know that you do want and need love. We all do. But in order to make room for it to arrive into your life, you must release the attachment you have to getting it; you must release the need for love. The needing part is taking up valuable energy and space in your life, yet it has no practical function; it's not getting you closer to the love.

What does get you closer is your behavior, and letting go of anything from your past that is lingering in your present and creating insecurity or ill will. Remember, what is in the past cannot be changed and shouldn't be kept alive. When you keep it alive by constantly revisiting it and fearing it will recur, you practically guarantee that it will. You create your very own self-fulfilling prophecy.

Your past may indeed have some unpleasant experiences. But they should be distant memories now, even if they occurred yesterday, as yesterday has no power over today except the power you give it. If you continue to feel resentment and the need for revenge, if you continue to refuse to forgive those who have wronged you, you allow your precious mind—which creates your precious life—to be filled with negativity. And, according to the Law of Attraction, that will make you a magnet for the negativity of others.

Instead of putting your attention on needing love or feeling like a doomed victim of your past, put your attention on loving yourself. Only when you truly love yourself do you attract others who are capable of and willing to love you.

LEARNING TO LOVE YOURSELF
FROM THE OUTSIDE IN

Sometimes you have to learn to love yourself from the outside in, meaning you need to fake it till you make it. Each day, I suggest you look at yourself in the mirror and say the following positive affirmations:

- I love myself.
- I approve of myself.
- I accept everything about myself.
- I forgive all who have hurt me.
- I love life and experience it to the fullest.
- I enjoy the people around me.
- I enjoy my work.
- I am grateful for my home.
- I welcome and graciously accept compliments.

If you have a problem looking in the mirror, I suggest you get a tube of lipstick and draw a smiley face so that every time you look in the mirror you smile. This will add to the effectiveness of your positive affirmations.

I guarantee that if you begin and end each day with these affirmations, your subconscious mind will have no choice but to create the circumstances and the feelings that will make them a reality.

Love, as they say, is a verb; it's something you do. Each moment of each day, you can be love and invite love by treating others the way you would like to be treated. The Golden Rule is timeless and all of us should live by it. This includes refraining from criticizing someone, even if you are in the right, finding ways to word what you want to say so it is the least hurtful, and being upset with the unpleasant behavior of your loved ones rather than with your loved ones themselves. It includes open, honest, kind communication, and active listening. And it includes compassion.

MY EXPERIENCE OF LOVE

What makes us love one person and not another? How do we learn to love? From our parents or from the person who raised us. Love is really learned behavior that you acquire between birth and nine-years old. The behavior you experienced created a map in your subconscious mind that dictates the way you respond today.

I grew up with loving parents that I feel presented me with many good examples of love and marriage. I fell in love with the "one," as young girls intend to do, and I fully trusted and loved my first husband. But I soon discovered that the best part of my marriage was the wedding. Seven months after the wedding, I found out my husband had a drinking problem, and that problem soon resulted with him beating me. After a week in the hospital I decided to go back home with him because he had me so convinced that I was so ugly he was the only person that could ever love me.

Within a month, the scene started to repeat itself. Lucky for me, one night he tripped over a coffee table and knocked himself unconscious. As I was lying in bed crying, I realized that no one deserved to be beaten. Suddenly, through the tears, the positive programming Dorothy had taught me emerged. But under it all was the belief system that you stick it out because marriage isn't something you give up on.

I decided to listen to the voice inside me that told me I was worth more than I was getting, and I left. The information in this chapter is what I worked with to restore my map to be able to allow someone else into my life. Someone healthier for me. And it worked.

ACTION STEP

MODELING LOVE

(Record your thoughts and feelings if that helps you.)

- Who represents healthy self-love and healthy love of others to you?
- Close your eyes and imagine that person.
- Envision how the person stands, how they walk, and how they use their hands and eyes.
- Imagine that person interacting with others. What does their voice sound like? What do they look like when they're listening? Observe how the other people react to your loving person.
- Imagine yourself standing close to your confident person. How do you feel? Can you feel their love?
- Imagine watching that person with their partner or spouse. What do they look like when they gaze into that person's eyes? What body language tells you they're in love?
- Pretend you're a human sponge and soak up the love of your model.
- Turn to the people in your vision and watch them react to you the same way they reacted to your loving person. Feel their respect and admiration, and feel your charisma and

confidence. Feel compassion and love.

* Now, open your eyes.

ACTION STEP

Fill-in Section #6 of Your *DISCOVER* Outcome Development Board

Cut out and paste photos and words that represent your model of Love onto section #6 of the Outcome Development Board from your Toolkit (or your own poster) and record your thoughts and feelings if that helps you.

Here are some tips for choosing the most effective images:

* Look for images of couples looking at each other lovingly.
* If you already have a beloved, paste a photo of that person on your poster.
* What kind of body language represents love to you? Choose images that depict people with that body language.
* If there are things (e.g., an engagement ring or a wedding chapel) that represent the kind of love you want, include them, too. Refrain from concentrating heavily on things, however.

ACTION STEP

USE HYPNOSIS TO TURBO-CHARGE YOUR LOVE

After you've done what you can on the conscious level to increase your self-love and attract love from others, it's time to turbo-charge your progress by enlisting the subconscious by way of hypnosis, which as always will begin with Instant Alpha Conditioning. After that you can either read the love script each time, record your own CD with the script, or listen to the "Love" CD in the Perfect Enough CD series. Just make sure you follow through so that the information is recorded in your brain. This will allow you to make the changes that will attract Love in your life. Remember you are worth it!

Let's turbo-charge your true desire to be happy with love right now!

INSTANT ALPHA CONDITIONING

Instructions:

1. Read each night, before retiring, for 21 nights. Read aloud, with feeling. Use the word you choose to replace the longer Alpha Conditioning and let Alpha easily occur.
2. Proceed immediately to the script for Love.

S	M	T	W	Th	F	Sat

From this moment on, each and every time I desire to attain the deep state of total relaxation, I am instantly and fully relaxed, as I am now drifting into the Alpha state of consciousness. The moment I think my chosen word _____, Alpha occurs. This word has an effect only when I use it and only under the proper circumstances. Each and every time I do use it, I am fully prepared to receive positive, beneficial and constructive suggestions, impressing each one deeper into my storage and memory facility of my brain.

From this moment on, _____ triggers deep relaxation of my mind and body. I feel Alpha occur. I feel wonderful. I feel comfortable. I am totally receptive and responsive to my own creative ideas and suggestions. I am bathed in a glow of quietness, peace, and serenity. My chosen word works only when I deliberately use it for deep relaxation to attain Alpha consciousness. Its use in regular conversation has no effect on me whatsoever. From this moment on, each and every time I desire the deep state of total relaxation, I am instantly and fully relaxed upon saying _____. Because my subconscious must follow my command, each and every time I desire total relaxation, I am instantly and fully relaxed when I think my chosen word_____. I feel a deep sense of gratification as this word programming becomes a reality. Feeling wonderful, generous, alive, and eager to develop healthy, lasting, love relationships . . .

LOVE

As I relax once more, I release every fearful experience of the past that relates to me loving myself or anyone else, and everything connected with those experiences. I find it easy to let go of my fears. I am a part of life, as we all are. We all move, live, and think, as we have a right to. Life goes on, and so do I, growing rich in experience and in capacity to achieve. My positive experiences supply me with a directness to meet the challenges of my life. All I must do is use the amazing power of my subconscious mind. I am using that capacity now to disengage myself from every negative, destructive, and harmful impression ever made upon me. They fade, fade, fade out of my life forever.

I am grateful and thankful for every experience of the past. I am now forgiving myself for every mistake I have ever made; and I forgive everyone else who may have in any way harmed me. I know that out of each experience, as I understand it, good must surely come to me. I forgive myself and move toward greater opportunity and greater achievement. I grow stronger with each experience and I am stronger than anything life can offer. I am preparing myself to meet life's challengers directly, free of negative conditioning. I am more than any challenge, for I possess the power and the ability to channel any experience into a rich and rewarding way of life.

As I do a release and clear processing with my imagination, I imagine, visualize myself at the beach. It is a beautiful day and I am safe and secure and feel totally okay. As I perceive myself at the beach there is a comfortable breeze and I can hear the ocean waves in the background. And now very, very vividly, I am fantasizing that I am digging a deep hole in the sand. I am digging deeper and deeper. When the hole is big enough and deep enough, I start putting in the hole all my negative, fear-based emotions. So now as I visualize this I am making it as real as possible. I am perceiving every detail of this movie in my mind. I am playing the role. I am playing the part and I am experiencing burying each fear in my mind. I smell the sand and the sea. I take a moment and allow this to happen in my mind, and now I have just seen my own reality. I have thrown away all the negativity and the fears. I have thrown away all the fear-based emotions. I am now open to new suggestions, which I will accept and act upon. I am now open to all the warmth, joy and fulfillment that life has to offer. I feel glad to be alive and enthusiastic about my future. I am now calm and relaxed and a sense of peace permeates my body and mind.

Now I fully have released past fears and all their effects on me. I am free, free of the past fear of love, free to be me, entirely. I accept myself completely. I am a valuable and talented human being and I am always aware of my innate worth. There are things to be done by me that are done better by me than by any other human being. Every word, every movement, every gesture of mine preserves my unique stamp upon life. There is no one who can exactly duplicate me. I am pleased, I accept myself, and I love myself. I am grateful for my new level of understanding.

I feel the emotion of warmth spreading calm throughout my body. As I use my imagination, I see myself outdoors and the sun is shining brightly overhead and I feel safe and secure. I feel the warmth of the sun on the top of my head, moving down to the tip of my toes, radiating out throughout my entire body to all my muscles, like a warm blanket of relaxation, moving down from the top of my head to the tips of my toes.

The reason I am reading this session is that I wish to increase my awareness of love and my ability to love others. I have decided that I am worthy of love and that I have a lot of love to give to the special people in my life. That's right! Good.

Now I visualize a symbol of love. The symbol of love is a circle, and each and every time I see a circle or think of a circle, thoughts of love are reactivated and work on my behalf. I allow love to flow into me, around me, and out into the world. Every cell is permeated with a glowing feeling of love, satisfying the deep longing within me, attracting love to me the gentle love of acceptance. I accept myself as a lovable person. I have the ability to express and receive love. I love others and I know that I am like a magnet building love within myself, and as the love grows I attract unconditional love to me. This process is perfectly summarized in the simple form of a circle.

I express love at the level I intuitively know others will accept. I give those I love freedom to be themselves with honor, and because that love is unconditional, they return it gratefully to me. What I want for myself, I want for everyone else, as I know that everyone is made of the same substance. We are all part of one great life. In that life we all live and move and have our own power of being. Since this is true, I forgive myself now for every mistake I have ever made. I let them be released at this very deep level from every cell of my being. I allow that release now and as I do, a new level of understanding of life begins to flow into my awareness. I am prepared for life and love living it.

I allow this new understanding to permeate my cells, to fill me with caring, with compassion, with love. I know that out of each experience I have had in life, good, understanding, and growth, has filled my awareness. I completely forgive myself now and as I also forgive all those who have in any way harmed me. I let this forgiveness enrich me. My new level of love awareness now enriches my every thought, word, and deed, and as I develop a love of giving out joy, of creation, and the satisfaction of using my inherent powers to accomplish something within me, something worthwhile is increased. That something is love awareness and it grows within. And like the sun expresses warmth, I express love, love, love to all those who come within me awareness. I radiate and share my love just by being me.

My expression of love enriches, enhances, amplifies, creates and develops people and situations. I experience a fulfillment of life, and my mature expression of love frees those I love to develop their own inner powers toward fulfillment. I allow those I love most deeply the chance to be themselves to express life according to their own potentials. Freeing them automatically frees me to be more creative, spontaneous, and enthusiastic while pursuing my own destiny. Life thus becomes a joy that I find myself appreciating immensely. As I move through life achieving, I look closely and deliberately at myself and ask, as many times as is necessary: "Am I moving in this direction with love in my heart?" When I find that love center, I move with strength and the satisfaction of knowing the path is correct for me. Love creates joy, strength. It joins others in peace, with honor. Love is my guide, my companion.

The circle perpetuates, strengthens and overflows to all who require love and unconditional caring. Love reflects me the giver. Love listens to its own inner voice. Love recognizes itself, it sees, it looks, it listens as well as hears. It touches and revels in gentle loving touch, a caress of true understanding on the intuitive level. I am feeling and receiving with my power of intention. This love is forgiving, asking nothing in return, giving from the abundance within me for now right now, love is instructed to grow and be in every cell of my being. Something of value replacing the useless tension I have now released. Something of value, love, unconditional love, left free, finding its own path, setting its own pace, traveling its own way in dignity, and uniqueness. Love needs no recognition. It simply is.

The circle reflects that love and each time I see one either inside or outside of my own awareness, the circle activates each idea presented here. I am instructing my deeper mind to allow the love within me to grow until I am able to give love unconditionally. For true giving is giving, and asking nothing in return. Love needs no recognition. It simply is. Joy is always an integral part of loving. There is joy in every act of life. When we allow the awareness of love to grow within our being, to work in love is to work in joy to live in love is to live in joy. I may not have before me the most creative and satisfying day to live, but I know that I must live it, I make the choice, and I choose to use the day in energy, enthusiasm, and determination to allow it to be the best day of my life.

I choose. More and more readily each time that I see a circle, the positive, love-filled experience. Love builds daily within my mind creating more and more fulfilling decisions. I choose from the heart, from love. Love is accepting the other person unconditionally. Realizing that today is an opportunity to change, to reflect the love, I have given out. Love is constantly watching, listening, waiting, feeling, adjusting, readjusting, and changing. Love shares, love frees, and love promotes growth and competence. Love reaches beyond where we are and creates warmth, acceptance, unconditional caring. Love is a catalyst for security within. The release of dormant energy. A gift unto mankind. Circles everywhere. Circles of love. Circles of caring. Circles are gifts. Love energy grows within me. I allow it to happen. I experience the love, the circle of love, a gift, a love imprint. I let it change my life.

This entire suggestion is represented by the letter "V" of my sub-key word "Discover." Anytime I think, say, or see the word "Discover," all suggestions keyed to this word are automatically activated, stimulated and work for my benefit.

You now have the choice to either awaken or to drift off into a normal, natural sleep. If you are going to awaken, say:

Twenty minutes. Wide awake.

If you are going to drift off into a normal, natural sleep, say:

I am now going to drift off into a normal, natural sleep. When I awaken, I will feel fully rested, calm, and at peace with myself, the world, and those around me.

CHAPTER 10

KEY #7: PROSPERITY

FROM SCARCITY TO ABUNDANCE

*Prosperity in the form of wealth works exactly the same as every-
thing else. You will see it coming into your life when you are
unattached to needing it.*
—Wayne Dyer

pros per i ty (pro-**sper**-i-tee)

noun

1. a successful, flourishing, or thriving condition, esp. in financial
   respects; good fortune.

MONEY IS A GREAT teacher. It is a vehicle for self-discovery,
self-improvement, and self-growth. Most people begin their
descent into dysfunction when they regard prosperity as having solely
to do with money; they forget that success in relationships and in
purpose and in work are all part of being prosperous.

Another popular aspect of prosperity dysfunction is attaching a
high (and random) dollar figure to wealth. Doing so sets you up for
failure and disappointment, because anything below your number
will equal poverty, unworthiness, and inadequacy.

Something that many people find surprising is that, for the most
part, happiness is not affected by where you are on the financial

spectrum. People who live from paycheck-to-paycheck are often just as happy, if not more, than people whose retirements are fully funded. So what exactly is prosperity, and how can you get some? As with all other aspects of discovering your true self, it involves facing your fears and reprogramming your mind.

What fears are keeping you from achieving prosperity?
- Fear of not having enough money for life's basic needs.
- Fear of not having enough money for "wants."
- Fear of not being able to keep up/measure up to others in your social circle.
- Fear that luck will run out.
- Fear of achieving a state of prosperity, then losing it.

As in every other chapter, I'm going to tell you that prosperity is a choice. Yes, it's a state of consciousness. In fact, everything is a state of consciousness. But it is also something you can choose to have. You can choose abundance. After all, whatever you believe, you will manifest.

You're first step, then, is to examine your current beliefs about prosperity, and about having what you desire. This isn't easy, as we all have issues with money, worthiness, shame, entitlement, and blame that swirl around in our heads and prevent us from a healthy relationship with the idea of wealth.

In my experience, there are three types of relationships with money:

* *You have it and feel guilty about it.*

People who have inherited wealth often feel guilty because they "haven't done anything to deserve it." This guilt can manifest itself in many ways, including: spending sprees to "get rid of" the money; other compulsive behaviors, such as gambling; giving money away without a plan; and constantly attracting people who "take" the money away. As long as you hold on to guilt about having money, you will never be at peace with it, and you'll constantly invite opportunities to spend it in irresponsible ways.

* *You want it but you don't believe you are worthy of it or could ever have it.*

People who don't think they are worthy of money often act so stingy that they will never attract any money. Remember, you get back what you put out. If you have a poverty consciousness, poverty will follow you. People with feelings of unworthiness will also manage to not get promoted; they won't follow their passions and dreams (because they're sure they'll fail); and they surround themselves with people who reinforce their unworthiness.

* *You get it and you keep losing it.*

The good news is that if you've attracted wealth to you in the past, you know you can do it again. The bad news is that anyone who has lost a fortune once—and especially more than once—probably didn't ever feel comfortable with the wealth. This is true even if they earned it themselves. If you didn't have a good role model for how to handle money, and you're the first person in your family to earn a substantial amount of money (or even win it), there is a high probability that you will somehow lose it. *Why?*

A HEALTHY RELATIONSHIP
WITH MONEY IS LEARNED

If no one ever taught you financial literacy or presented you with a good example of how to deal with money, it wouldn't be surprising if you had difficulty making or keeping it. If your parents had a poverty consciousness and were withholding with money, chances are you will not grow up thinking there is enough to go around.

Most people simply internalize and perpetuate whatever beliefs their parents displayed regarding money. In other words, if your parents lived in fear of running out of money, unless you have worked on your own relationship with money, you're likely to live in fear of running out of money, as well.

HOW TO BECOME FINANCIALLY LITERATE

There are hundreds of books that can help you understand how money works, both in the material world of saving and investing and giving, and in the more metaphysical world that includes the Law of Attraction. Authors like Suze Orman, David Bach, Jean Chatzky, and Jane Bryant Quinn have made a great living by explaining the basics of personal finance. Go to your local bookstore, to the personal finance section, and browse the books for the one that resonates with you. Stay away from the get-rich-quick books, and stick with the basics of financial literacy.

Whichever book you choose, many of the basic points will be the same. Authors differ on investment strategies and whether or not you should pay off your mortgage as soon as you can, but the fundamentals of handling money are the same. Some are:

- You need to take in more money than you spend each month. If you list all of your expenses and your income, and your expense total is more than your income total, go

through your expenses and eliminate or decrease the ones
you can alter (such as eating out, entertainment, cable,
subscriptions, hair, nails, and other non-necessities).

- Before you even think about any major purchases, you
  should be able to pay all of your bills each month, and that
  includes putting the maximum percentage allowable into
  your retirement account, and maintaining an emergency
  account that contains sufficient funds for six months of
  expenses. In cash.

- Start saving for retirement as early as possible, because
  you'll have to save much more money, much faster, as time
  goes on. (This is due to what is known as "the magic of
  compounding" and "the time value of money.")

- Distinguish between *wants* and *needs,* and consider your
  retirement and your emergency fund *needs.* Only after you've
  allotted money for all of your needs, should you begin
  spending on your wants.

- Philanthropy should be a non-negotiable component of
  your financial plan. Remember, you get back what you put
  out.

WHAT DOES PROSPERITY MEAN TO YOU?

Yes, money is an important part of prosperity, and developing
a healthy relationship with money is vital to achieving prosperity,
regardless of your definition. But prosperity includes abundance of
all kinds: love, good fortune, career success, family success, and good
health.

If you think of prosperity the way you think of perfection—as a
state to always strive to but never to reach, you will position yourself
to always fall short. You must define prosperity as the abundance of

material, personal, and spiritual wealth that you are entitled. You must fully believe you deserve your prosperity.

Like any other goal, prosperity must not only be defined, but you must have a clear picture of what it looks like so your subconscious can work its magic and make your picture a reality. What are some images that represent abundance to you? Can you see them in full color? Can you smell and taste them? Imagine abundance, believe abundance, use the language of abundance, and abundance will find you.

One of my most interesting client-stories with regard to prosperity is a wonderful young woman whom I'll call Claire. Claire grew up with a lot of problems and mixed messages about money. One message was that she needed a higher education in order to succeed. And with a great education under her belt, she fulfilled that message by always getting good jobs as a salesperson and making a decent living.

She wanted more, though. Yes, she had a great job and great potential, but she wasn't feeling prosperous. And she certainly wasn't manifesting abundance. She started listening to my Sales CD from my Corporate Series, and concluded it "wasn't working" after there was no change in her income. She called to complain, and I suggested that she come in to see me for a session. When she arrived and we began talking, it became clear that she had a lack of self-confidence. But she also had some other issue that wasn't clear yet. When I asked her about the messages she received as a child, an important one emerged: that salespeople are "pushy," "aggressive," and "sleazy."

There was Claire, working as a salesperson, with a brain full of negative associations to the word "salesperson." It was no wonder she wasn't manifesting abundance. If she did, that would mean she was a salesperson. If she did, that would mean she was pushy, aggressive, and sleazy.

With a little hypnosis, most people can reprogram their minds and turn their negative and limiting beliefs around. What are some of your limiting beliefs around wealth?

- I believe I don't deserve it.
- I believe I will never make more than $100,000 in a year.
- I believe that whenever I get money, I somehow manage to lose it.
- I believe I'm not good with money.
- I believe I'm not a lucky person.
- I believe that a certain amount of money will make me happy.

As of this moment, put those beliefs in a mental drawer and label it, "the past." Remember, as long as it look place one second ago, it took place in the past.

From now on, you're beliefs about wealth will manifest because you will visualize them, support them with words and thoughts, and create them with your actions.

- Visualize the life you desire.
- Visualize your achievements, your enthusiasm, and your satisfaction for continually reaching and surpassing your goals.
- Visualize yourself grateful for your many blessings, including your wonderful friends and family, and your meaningful job that compensates you well.
- Visualize yourself paying each of your bills as soon as they arrive, and having a large, positive balance in your account after you've paid all of your bills and even contributed to your retirement account and your emergency savings account (where you already have enough money to pay six month's worth of expenses).
- Visualize this life of yours. Allow your imagination to

create every detail. Remember, your mind doesn't know
the difference between what's real and what's imaginary, so
when you imagine your life, you create it.

- Visualize only your outcome—not the details of how you
  reached your goal. Why? Because if you get bogged down
  in the details, you tell the world that the way to prosperity
  that you are describing is *the only way* it'll happen for you.
  Imagining the process can actually stop you from fulfilling
  your destiny. Concentrate on the end product, and let the
  universe find the best way for you to get it.

There are many practical things you can do to develop a prosperity
consciousness. For instance, reciprocity and generosity are vital
components of abundance. When you give liberally and freely, without
strings, you tell the world that you believe there is more than enough
for everyone, and you're happy to be a vehicle for other people's
abundance. And, of course, because of the Law of Attraction, the more
generous you are, the more generosity you will attract. The same is
true of reciprocity. The ability to freely, joyfully give back when you are
gifted with something, increases the probability that you will always
be in a position of reciprocating (therefore, you are always being gifted
with things). And when I say you are being gifted, I don't just mean
with money. The rules of reciprocity and generosity are equally true
of kindness, giving someone a break, and sharing material wealth.
Because we are all part of the same energy, we are always giving and
receiving energy. *What kind of energy are you giving and receiving?*

One of the keys to developing prosperity is to begin by giving.
Waiting to receive is stingy and tells the world that you don't think
there's enough for everyone. Here are some ways you can give of
yourself, starting today:

- No matter what your job is, do it with passion and give all you have.
- Donate to your favorite charity. My grandmother taught me to always tithe 15% of my income. I haven't always made that, but I always manage to balance it out by volunteering my time, which sometimes is even more valuable to the person or organization I'm giving to.
- Volunteer your time with a local community organization.
- Call your mother and/or your father and tell them how much you love and appreciate them.
- Surprise someone who ordinarily takes care of you with a home-cooked dinner.
- Give money to someone who needs it, and don't expect it back.
- Be especially kind to people in service positions, such as wait staff and checkout people.
- Release the need to want payback from those you think "owe you."
- Practice your attitude of gratitude for the many gifts you have.
- Look in the mirror every morning and tell yourself that all good things you do come back to you tenfold (or more!).
- Money is the only entity you will be in relationship with for your entire life. There aren't even any people you can necessarily say that about. Every day, be thankful for the money that is in your life.
- Be grateful for all of the challenging people in your life who help you grow.

ACTION STEP

MODEL PROSPERITY

(Record your experience of this process if that helps you.)

- Who represents prosperity for you?
- Close your eyes and imagine that person.
- Envision how the person stands, how they walk, and how they use their hands and eyes. Listen to that person speak. Watch that person drive their car to their home.
- Imagine that person interacting with others. What does their voice sound like? What kinds of things do they frequently say to describe their career and relationships? Observe how the other people react to your person who speaks well of their life, yet isn't boastful. Observe how content your prosperous person is.
- Imagine yourself standing close to the person you'd like to model. How do you feel? Can you feel their contentment?
- Pretend you're a human sponge and soak up all their prosperity and confidence.
- Turn to the people in your vision and watch them react to you the same way they reacted to the person you're modeling. Feel the respect and admiration from those around you.
- Now, open your eyes.

ACTION STEP

Fill-in Section #7 of Your *DISCOVER* Outcome Development Board

Cut out and paste photos and words that represent your model of Prosperity onto section #7 of the Outcome Development Board from your Toolkit (or your own poster), and record your thoughts and feelings of this process if that helps you.

Here are some tips for choosing the most effective images:

- Choose outcomes that represent material wealth, but don't stop there. What else does prosperity mean to you? Does it mean a clean bill of health? If so, create one and paste it onto your board.

- Be careful with limiting thoughts such as, "I'd like to have a bigger house, but what could I possibly to do ever afford that? It's not realistic!" Forget about what you think is realistic. The universe works, and if you believe in your outcome, the universe will find a way to produce it.

ACTION STEP

Use Hypnosis to Turbo-charge Your New Prosperity and Abundance

All of the above are actions you can take with your conscious mind. If you practice them daily, they will become habits, and your prosperity consciousness will begin to make it known by sending you opportunities, gifts, ideas, and support for your goals and dreams. Now it's time to turbo charge your conscious efforts by enlisting your subconscious mind, which will help make everything flow even more easily. You can read the self-hypnosis script, record the script in your own voice or you can listen to the *Perfect Enough* CD called "Prosperity and Abundance". It is up to you! Just make sure you program the information into the subconscious mind.

Now, let's retrain your brain to attract to you what you want!

Instructions:

1.   Read each night, before retiring, for 21 nights. Read aloud, with feeling, using the word you chose earlier to replace the longer version of Alpha Conditioning.

2.   Proceed immediately to the script for Prosperity and Abundance.

S	M	T	W	Th	F	Sat

From this moment on, each and every time I desire to attain the deep state of total relaxation, I am instantly and fully relaxed, as I am now drifting into the Alpha state of consciousness. The moment I think my chosen word _____, Alpha occurs. This word has an effect only when I use it and only under the proper circumstances. Each and every time I do use it, I am fully prepared to receive positive, beneficial and constructive suggestions, impressing each one deeper into my storage and memory facility of my brain.

From this moment on, _____ triggers deep relaxation of my mind and body. I feel Alpha occur. I feel wonderful. I feel comfortable. I am totally receptive and responsive to my own creative ideas and suggestions. I am bathed in a glow of quietness, peace, and serenity. My chosen word works only when I deliberately use it for deep relaxation to attain Alpha consciousness. Its use in regular conversation has no effect on me whatsoever. From this moment on, each and every time I desire the deep state of total relaxation, I am instantly and fully relaxed upon saying _____. Because my subconscious must follow my command, each and every time I desire total relaxation, I am instantly and fully relaxed when I think my chosen word_____ _____. I feel a deep sense of gratification as this word programming becomes a reality. Feeling wonderful, generous, alive, and eager to enhance my prosperity . . .

PROSPERITY AND ABUNDANCE

I visualize myself as a positive happy person. I am a kind person. I accept abundance in my life and I visualize what I want and it is allowed to materialize. I expect prosperity in my life personal and financially.

I use my money wisely. I give of myself, my time, and my love. I allow my inner mind to let go of any and all past fears of money. I allow my mind to expand and see my ability to achieve my intentions easily like an eagle in the sky. I see that eagle in the sky lifting itself higher and higher as it soars in the sky. In utter silence and contentment, the wind currents lift the eagle higher and higher. Knowledge fills my mind that I too can rise above any previous limitation. I am free, free to create. I am as free as the eagle, soaring high in the soft blue sky. I have all I need to allow prosperity to happen. I have all I need to open all opportunity to attract to me through the Law of Attraction. I believe that what I can perceive I can achieve. I am honest, I am enthusiastic, I am intelligent, and I am disciplined.

I am an individual who thinks before I react. I perform all my skills with a particular purpose in mind. There are rewards to each and every one of my actions. I am able to envision the future rewards and benefits of my present course of action. I possess the skills to plan for my future success, for the success of my life. My life is enhanced each and every time I reap the rewards of my work. These rewards make me even more motivated to enjoy life to the fullest.

I imagine and see myself enjoying life on a higher and happier level. I allow myself see a large image of myself at my very best. This image is the way I want to be, it is an image of how I once was, along with how I want to me. I allow myself to have the traits of that someone that I look up to. I see all the positive ideas that I have learned and read. I allow all the positive information on how money comes to me.

I see this image of me with my life force. It is easy for me to visualize, see, feel the vibration, the color and the sound of me achieving all of my outcomes. I am absorbing this image completely. I see me the way that I want to be. This is the person that I am.

This image is the very best "me" picture. I see this image as big as I can, this me, loving me, the best me I can possibly be. I am storing this in my mind as the very best "me" image.

Now I am imagining in my mind the objects of my desire. Good. Now, I see and visualize this image of me, the very best "me" along with the image of the objects of my desire. This final image brings me pleasure and increases my motivation to achieve more – at a higher level.

The symbol for this entire suggestion of prosperity and abundance in my life is the eagle. The eagle is often seen as money. It is a symbol of greatness and abundance. I feel secure in the knowledge that wealth is mine. My inner mind obeys my commands. Through the Law of Attraction, the universe provides me through my power of intention. I desire financial success, I deserve financial success, and I receive financial success. I desire an abundant supply of money. I desire money so that I can live a richer, more abundant life of greater self-expression and greater achievement. I create the outcomes and I live them, easily and naturally.

I am a kind and generous person. I expect wealth to come to me. I use my money wisely. I give of myself, my time, my money, and my love. I am an outgoing, loving and generous person. As I seek to do more good for others, all the channels of life, people, situations, and conditions pour out a greater abundance to me. Success exists for me; I have the right to it. I express life in a full and wholesome way.

I attract money. Money flows to me easily, freely, and generously. I see myself living richly and luxuriously. My heart is open to give out. My hands are open to receive. I pay my bills joyously because it means I have obtained something of value in exchange for my money. My success is steady and constant. As I grow in understanding, I prosper. Wealth is mine now. I accept it. I am grateful for it. I am pleased with my achievements.

In my imagination, I now visualize myself as a powerful magnet, attracting that which I desire in ever-increasing abundance. As I grow in understanding, in kindness, and in generosity, my mind opens to create the means to obtain, in fantastic profusion, the things money can buy. I enjoy my success. I have a right to it. I deserve it. I share my prosperity, my abundance, and my love with others. I am open to giving and I am open to receiving. From the magnificent abundance within, gained from having served myself so well, I am free to express love, generosity, and happiness. These emotions flow freely from me, for I have much to give.

These wonderful thoughts fill me with boundless energy and enthusiasm. These thoughts bring a smile to my face, and feelings of security in my inner self. My self-confidence increases and I am certain that I will attain all of my outcomes. My ambition and the energy I stir in others is contagious. I deserve to achieve even greater success. I allow it to happen.

Commitment and persistence are everywhere in my life. My communication skills are effective. I like working with others and sharing my ideas with them. Communication is the key to me working well with others in the workplace and at home. I am an effective communicator. When other people communicate their ideas to me, I respect their opinions. I take time to comment to others and my reactions are always appropriate. The way I work with others helps me gain financial prosperity and abundance with ease.

I love what I do. And I do what I love. I love my life so much. The prosperity and abundance I obtain from my life makes my life fun and exciting. Other people notice how much I enjoy my life. I practice, achieve and maintain balance in my life. Balance between my job and my personal life happens automatically. That's right, I let it happen. Balance is the key to maintaining the success that I have achieved. My life automatically is in a state of balance.

I am a positive individual. Positive energy is infused into all that

I do. I speak well of myself and of my prosperity. Others speak well of me too. I am a natural leader. People enjoy being around me and saying that they know me. My positive energy is contagious. Other people feel the positive energy that emanates from me and my life. When the opportunity exists, I praise others and others praise me.

I am open to give and I am open to receive from the magnificent abundance I gain from having served myself well. I am free to express generosity and happiness. As I relax deeper and deeper, I continue to allow my inner mind to set me free, free as an eagle in the sky. My abundance is lifting with the wind currents, higher and higher in utter silence and contentment. I possess the knowledge that I too can rise above any limitation. I am free, free as an eagle soaring high in the soft blue sky.

My symbol for prosperity and abundance is the eagle. The eagle is a symbol of quietness, greatness and secure abundance. I feel secure with the knowledge that this wealth is mine. My inner mind obeys my command each and every time I see an eagle or think of an eagle. Anchored into my mind every time I see an eagle in or out of my conscious awareness, this program multiplies in my mind. I am aware of this strong, vibrant image of prosperity and abundance that is triggered within my deeper mind and I feel secure and serene in the knowledge that I truly allow financial success to be in my life. I am a financial success.

I have a wonderful sense of gratitude for all that I am, I feel secure with the knowledge that wealth is mine and I am a financial success.

This entire suggestion is represented by the letter "E" of my sub-key word "Discover." Anytime I think, say, or see the word "Discover," all suggestions keyed to this word are automatically activated, stimulated and work for my benefit.

You now have the choice to either awaken or to drift off into a normal, natural sleep. If you are going to awaken, say:

Twenty minutes. Wide awake.

If you are going to drift off into a normal, natural sleep, say:

I am now going to drift off into a normal, natural sleep. When I awaken, I will feel fully rested, calm, and at peace with myself, the world, and those around me.

CHAPTER 11

KEY #8: MEANING
FROM INSIGNIFICANCE TO PURPOSE

Many people have a wrong idea of what constitutes
true happiness. It is not attained through self-gratification,
but through fidelity to a worthy purpose.
—Helen Keller

pur pose (pur p*uh* s)
noun
1. The reason for which something exists or is done, made, used, etc.

THAT'S ONE POWERFUL DEFINITION. Your purpose is the reason for which you exist. Those of you who have found your purpose no doubt are comfortable with the idea. But those of you who haven't are, I'm sure, a bit intimidated. But have no fear, with a little work you can find meaning in your life beyond your day-to-day existence. And if you're feeling at all resistant, at the center of your hesitation is probably a fear of some kind. Here are some fears that might be keeping you from unearthing the profound meaning that's just waiting for you to recognize it:

- Fear that you'll die without having contributed.
- Fear that life is ultimately meaningless.

- Fear that other people know the secret of life and you don't.
- Fear that when you think you've found your meaning, you'll be wrong.
- Fear that it will involve too much work or change.

Do you have any of those fears? Can you articulate the purpose of your life in one sentence? Are you being called to do something, yet you ignore that calling? If so, what is that calling and what's so terrifying about acknowledging it?

In my experience, every single person has an inkling—a conscious inkling—about what they should be doing to make their life more meaningful. And once I peer into their subconscious minds (along with them, of course), we discover that the inkling is more of an urge or a need. Each of my clients feels a deep-seated need to make meaning of their lives. And the best part is, they know what they need to do. All they're missing is the how and the when.

If you're not sure where your meaning lies, here's a hint: Don't follow the money. In other words, if you're doing something that makes your heart and soul sing everyday (in your job), you'd know it. Otherwise, you've probably got the wrong job. But worry not; you don't necessarily have to change your life completely.

Everyone has one issue that drives most of their behavior. For some people, that one thing is perfection in their home. Or money. Or beauty. Or mastery of something physical, like the triathlon. These are all socially-acceptable goals and purposes, but they won't feed your soul and they won't give your life significance. I promise. What's behind all of these behaviors, which are technically compulsions, is an emptiness and a fear that you will not have significance or be remembered. And that, my friends, is not what I mean when I say we all need to find our purpose.

FINDING YOUR PURPOSE

Take a moment to relax your mind and body. Close your eyes.

- Make a mental image of what you would call happiness in your life. What does it involve?
- Imagine what you're grateful for. What is it?
- What makes you feel the most at peace?
- What are you the most proud of?
- What did you wish you could do more of, but you think you don't have enough time?
- Whether you believe in a personal God who intervenes when you pray, or a creator God who created everything and is now observing as it all unfolds, you are, as they say, not a human having spiritual experiences, but a spirit having human experiences. We are all, first and foremost, a soul that was put here for a reason. What might your reason be?

Some people experience an *ah-ha* with this kind of exercise, and others do not. For the latter, the reason is that it is a conscious exercise, and there are all kinds of obstacles your mind has set up to prevent you from realizing your significance.

ACTION STEP

THE EULOGY EXERCISE

What do you want to be when you grow up? Who do you want to be? Let's create your future self (and by future, I simply mean not this present moment) by starting from the end of your life and working backward.

1. Relax, close your eyes, and visualize your own funeral. Spare no expense with the flower arrangements, the location,

the clothes you're wearing, and the coffin, if you want one. Imagine who is there and what their faces look like. Are they devastated? Are they content? Are they the faces proud to be at the funeral of their loved one who had a life well lived and worth living?

2. Imagine that five people will eulogize you: your spouse or partner, your child (real or imagined), a sibling or other relative, someone you work with, and a member of your community. Imagine their eulogies and imagine their faces. Hear their voices. Observe the reactions from the rest of the gathering. Do they laugh? Do they cry? Do they all reminisce about your love of life, your sense of humor, and your compassion? What exactly do they talk about? Make a list of what you think they'll say if you were to die today. Then, make a list of what you want them to say about you. That second list—that, is your meaning.

3. What kind of behavior do you need to start exhibiting today in order to have the funeral and eulogies you desire? If, for instance, you would like a member of your community to say you are selfless and always looking to give voice to the voiceless, what would you have to do—on a consistent basis—to create that kind of assessment from a community member?

4. At many funerals, eventually the discussion comes around to one phrase that best describes the way the deceased lived his or her life. At your funeral, what will that phrase be? Do you want people to say, "Boy, that Jeanne Sullivan sure had great hair!" *No?* Well, what do you want them to say?

5. Your answer to #4 is your purpose. Now you have the opportunity to recreate your life according to that purpose. You must create objectives that will help you achieve your

purpose. In other words, for people to say, for instance, that you "Gave voice to the voiceless," what actions and behaviors do you have to exhibit? Make a list of them.

6. With your list in hand, it's time to make it reality. Each evening before you go to sleep, read your list and tell yourself that you are the person who gives voice to the voiceless. You are the person who does all of the things on your list. And each day, do one thing to bring yourself one step closer to becoming the new you. And in a couple of weeks or months, *presto,* you can become someone who gives voice to the voiceless.

Each time you do something—anything—you're telling the world a little bit about who you are. When you do your eulogy exercise and you begin to take action to fulfill your purpose, you're telling the world who you're becoming. This might be disconcerting to some people around you, as many people are not comfortable with change. Yet others will see you evolving and get angry because they take your behavior personally and interpret it as a challenge for them to step up and change, and they don't want to. Be prepared for resistance from yourself as well as the outside world. But be comforted by the reality that when you're changing, you're evolving. You're growing. You're becoming who you were meant to be.

MY PERSONAL STORY OF MEANING

Some people go through their lives living what *they think* is their meaning, then one day that all changes. I thought I would get my children into college and then work part-time at a local jewelry store and enjoy horseback riding as my hobby. Then when Dorothy passed away seven years ago, I stood and listened to everyone talk about her life at her funeral. Dozens of people spoke of what she had done and how much she'd helped them. And she had helped me, too. She had been like a second mother from whom I had learned a great deal. She never talked about all the good she had done, she lived by just being a wonderful example. Suddenly, I realized that life could have true meaning. Meaning meant to do what you love and to love what you do. And by doing you live in your own intention. It doesn't mean you have to set the world on fire or be famous, but that you work everyday doing something for others. Giving is necessary for meaning. Paying it forward is a requirement. Being the best you can be at whatever you choose to be.

I remember being a housewife and mom. Most of the time I didn't feel like I was enough because being a housewife really wasn't considered a career. But now that I have done that and now that I work full time, I must say that being the full-time mom was the hardest job ever. I thought that I was doing everything the right way, but lo and behold, things didn't always turn out the way I wanted.

Now each of my children had to discover their own way and their own intention. In my opinion I did the best I could. Yet, like every parent, I'm sure my kids blame a lot of stuff on me. I just trust that they will read this book and learn what they need from it.

I came home from the funeral and I set out on my quest to teach everyone that hypnosis is the greatest thing since sliced bread. I was dedicated to continuing the legacy that Dorothy had left behind.

I must explain something very important here. When I went to Omni Hypnosis School in Deland, Florida. I had a lot of obstacles to overcome. First, I didn't like the sound of my voice when recorded. Second, I couldn't speak in front of a crowd. And finally, I didn't think I could go into a room and hypnotize anyone. Well, after I was hypnotized to do all three, I earned many certifications and opened my company, Summit Dynamics LLC, like Dorothy's Spectra

Dynamics (and after my favorite place in this world, Lake Summit). I have recorded over 200 CDs that I sell well, I speak at many functions each year, and I hypnotize over 30 people a week. Once again I must say, you can do anything you want to do. I am living proof.

I set out to change the world and found my goal a lot more difficult than I had anticipated. I honestly felt that once someone heard my story, all of the right things would begin to happen. I asked friends to introduce me to their famous friends so that I could get my foot in the door. To my surprise, however, good friends of the famous don't ask favors of their famous friends. I would have to do everything myself, and work my way up from nothing, which is what I've done.

I now have reached a high level of success with my clients and with my business, but that success didn't come easily or without problems. I have borrowed a lot of money that, lucky for me, my husband is helping me pay back. I am not washing my dishes in the bathtub, nor am I homeless. I am just a normal person on a mission to help as many people as I can.

There are times when I feel like a broken record because I repeat myself so much. I tell people they must access their subconscious minds to create lasting change. I say they need to develop habit patterns that support the behavior and live the way they want to, so they can produce the life they want. But, broken record or not, I am fueled by my passion to fulfill my meaning. I am fueled by a passion to help as many people as I can, and all will eventually fall into place because I live my life with purpose—*on purpose.* Remember that I didn't get here by just reading books or going to therapy. Or by taking medication. I used my subconscious mind, and you should too.

As I sit and type today, I have had a new meaningful experience in my life. I attended a funeral yesterday. My sister's mother-in-law was a very jovial woman. She lived her life with a smile on her face and no matter what came her way she handled it with grace. As I listened to two of her grandsons (one being my nephew), I cried, for I felt such a true connection to how she was being talked about. Her traditions and happy way of always being reminded me of who I am, and who I want to continue being. The eulogy exercise took on a new meaning for me. The importance of it became so clear. It's like writing the script for your life and giving yourself back to yourself. So if you haven't done it make sure you take the time to do it and learn from it.

ACTION STEP

MODELING MEANING

(Record your thoughts and feelings if that helps you.)
- Who has found their purpose in their live and lives it with passion and joy?
- Close your eyes and imagine that person.
- Envision how the person stands, how they walk, and how they use their hands and eyes. Listen to that person speak. What do they spend their energy speaking about?
- Imagine that person interacting with others. What does their voice sound like? What kinds of things do they frequently say to describe their purpose? Observe how the other people react to your person who speaks well of their life.
- Imagine yourself standing close to the person you'd like to model. How do you feel? Can you feel their contentment? Can you feel the passion for their purpose?
- Pretend you're a human sponge and soak up all their good language and feelings.
- Turn to the people in your vision and watch them react to you the same way they reacted to the person you're

modeling. Feel the respect and admiration from those around you.

- Now, open your eyes.

ACTION STEP

FILL-IN SECTION #8 OF YOUR *DISCOVER* OUTCOME DEVELOPMENT BOARD

Cut out and paste photos and words that represent your model of Positive Meaning onto section #8 of the Outcome Development Board from your Toolkit (or your own poster), and record your thoughts and feelings about this process if that helps you.

Here are some tips for choosing the most effective images:
- The US has a history filled with philanthropists, yet some amassed their wealth in rather unsavory ways. Be careful in whom you choose.
- Philanthropists are generally thought of as individuals with massive personal or family wealth, yet some of history's most giving, loving individuals lived lives of poverty (think Mother Teresa of Calcutta). Include such humanitarians in your exploration of meaning.
- What are some objects that you feel help give your life meaning? Find images of those objects and paste them onto your poster.

ACTION STEP

USE HYPNOSIS TO TURBO-CHARGE YOUR MEANING

Now that you've done work on the conscious level, use self-hypnosis to turbo-charge your quest for and fulfillment of your meaning in life. As with any self-hypnosis script, you must relax yourself first by using Instant Alpha Conditioning. Remember you can choose to read the script every night, record and listen your own voice, or listen to the "Meaning" CD in the Perfect Enough CD Series. It is so important to follow through and complete the whole book. I have given you so much to do... Just remember that you are worth it!

Let's work with *your* powerful subconscious, and help you find your highest Meaning!

INSTANT ALPHA CONDITIONING

Instructions:

1. Use the word you selected to replace the longer version of the Alpha conditioning technique. Read the following script and let Alpha occur each night, before retiring, for 21 nights. Read aloud, with feeling.

2. Proceed immediately to the script for Meaning.

S	M	T	W	Th	F	Sat

From this moment on, each and every time I desire to attain the deep state of total relaxation, I am instantly and fully relaxed, as I am now drifting into the Alpha state of consciousness. The moment I think my chosen word _____, Alpha occurs. This word has an effect only when I use it and only under the proper circumstances. Each and every time I do use it, I am fully prepared to receive positive, beneficial and constructive suggestions, impressing each one deeper into my storage and memory facility of my brain.

From this moment on, _____ triggers deep relaxation of my mind and body. I feel Alpha occur. I feel wonderful. I feel comfortable. I am totally receptive and responsive to my own creative ideas and suggestions. I am bathed in a glow of quietness, peace, and serenity. My chosen word works only when I deliberately use it for deep relaxation to attain Alpha consciousness. Its use in regular conversation has no effect on me whatsoever. From this moment on, each and every time I desire the deep state of total relaxation, I am instantly and fully relaxed upon saying _____. Because my subconscious must follow my command, each and every time I desire total relaxation, I am instantly and fully relaxed when I think my chosen word_____ _____. I feel a deep sense of gratification as this word programming becomes a reality. Feeling wonderful, generous, alive, and eager to be on purpose. . .

MEANING

I have the energy and self-love that will enable me to begin the process of discovering my meaning. This energy is so strong and complete that I will be able to always point myself in the direction of my highest good. That's right. I will now have all of the courage and energy necessary to move towards my own highest good and I have a tremendous feeling of self-love inside my heart. As I realize this, I begin my process of self-discovery. A joyous celebration of all I am and all I become. I celebrate my own vital place inside the flow of the universe. Knowing that as I feel a part of the universe, I will never again feel alone. I know that everything that has been happening is actually part of a process enabling me to do what I have been meant to do all along. All that has been occurring around me has occurred to free me so I may find my meaning in life and in the world. I also find and create all I am meant to find and create. As I allow myself to become fully aware of this, I will be able to forgive all that has occurred. Inside this forgiveness, I find even more loving freedom. I may now go into a safe place inside myself. That's right. I find a path inside myself that leads to my own truth. I relax more with every word and I find a safe, secret place that is mine only. As I find myself on this path, I become aware of a wonderful feeling of energy that I feel now generating inside of my body. I feel a wonderful, warm energy moving through my body. I feel it traveling throughout my body, moving very slowly and comfortably. I allow positive energy inside my heart. The feeling moves through my heart and soul as I feel more and more comfortable. I find myself in a safe, secret place inside myself. Feeling so comfortable. Very good. Now I focus on true feeling. I allow a color-filled, positive energy to move through me. My inner self is directing me toward thoughts and images that will enable me to feel joy and happiness. My inner self will continually allow a feeling of comfort and encouragement to be a part of me discovering my meaning. I remind myself that all that occurs leads me toward my purpose. Now, I concentrate on the areas of my life that require attention. I focus on these areas and imagine a wave of energy is moving through them and allowing a sense of peace to saturate them. That's right. I am letting a feeling of harmony and balance be attached to these areas so I can explore the possibilities for my own meaning in life. I am a marvelous, self-healing mechanism and I am now actively creating my own well-being. I imagine myself outside in a beautiful garden. I feel comfortable. I notice that there are two small tables in this garden. I am relaxing more and more as I allow myself to go over to the table. On this table I notice there are two small blank books. I notice the cover of the book, it is called *The Book of Sadness*. I pick up the book and imagine I am writing in it all of the hurts of my entire life. That's right. I see myself writing in all the old negativity. The despair. The issues that can never be resolved. The grief. Any other emotions, thoughts, or details of the past that might prevent me from moving freely into a happy future. That's right. I jot down the dreams I had that I never allowed to manifest. I write it all down and notice how with each entry I am making in *The Book of Sadness*, I feel freer. That's right. I feel a sense of relief with each notation I make. Good. As I continue, when the time is right for me, I then move to the next step. I notice there's a large deep hole in the ground. And a shovel next to it. I imagine myself walking over to the hole in the ground and dropping *The Book of Sadness* into the hole. Next, I pick up the shovel and begin burying the disappointments and negative emotions of the past, one shovel-full at a time. That's right. At my own pace, I am able to let go of the past and to bury it one shovel-full at a time. It is time to finish burying the book.

Now I imagine the book has been completely buried. And now I realize during this time that I can examine the positive lessons I've learned from my past. There are a lot of positives I realize and I keep all of that information. I now consider that no matter what occurred in the past, I survived because I am a survivor. I realize, too, all the steps I took in the past have made me who I am today and that is Perfect Enough. And now the person I am today is truly a wonderful gift to the world. I am aware that I've learned positive lessons from my past, and I will now be able to move freely and joyously into the future to now discover my meaning. Wonderful. I imagine picking up the second book and noticing that the cover reads *The Book of Meaning*. But all of its pages are blank. There's a very important reason that the pages are blank; it is up to me to find my own meaning. I now decide to either repeat the past or to learn from it, and to take what I've learned into a brighter future. It's my choice and I am now beginning the process, now working with the **DISCOVER PROCESS**. In my *Book of Meaning*, I am creating a roadmap with the choices that will ensure my happiness, my health, and my total fulfillment. I see myself writing the chapters of my future. I write about my meaning in life and how I will make it so. I picture myself writing thoughts that come to me, letting my inner self and the highest truths and God dictate to me. All the things I will tell myself enable me to achieve my meaning. That's right.

Now I notice on the second table there are two bags. The first bag is full of grass seed. I see and feel myself sprinkling the grass seed over the fresh, pure, earth that covers *The Book of Sadness*. I feel myself pressing the seeds into the ground with my bare feet and toes. I notice the second bag contains three tulip bulbs: one red, one yellow, and one violet. I plant the red tulip bulb, knowing it represents the positive love that is about to grow in my heart. Now I plant the yellow tulip bulb, knowing it represents the positive health I will continually manifest in my body. Now I plant the violet tulip bulb, knowing it represents the positive life meaning that I am discovering for myself. I am fully aware I have planted positive love, positive health and positive life in the garden of my mind. These very things have already begun to grow inside me. Very good. Every time I become aware of my past, I have learned from it and I continually let go. I am always creating room inside myself for more love and happiness. I consider this and I feel love and joy growing inside me.

This entire suggestion is represented by the letter "R" of my sub-key word "Discover." Anytime I think, say, or see the word "Discover," all suggestions keyed to this word are automatically activated, stimulated and work for my benefit.

You now have the choice to either awaken or to drift off into a normal, natural sleep. If you are going to awaken, say:

Twenty minutes. Wide awake.

If you are going to drift off into a normal, natural sleep, say:

I am now going to drift off into a normal, natural sleep. When I awaken, I will feel fully rested, calm, and at peace with myself, the world, and those around me.

A FINAL WORD

Perfect Enough has been designed to help guide you to be the person you want to be, and *not* a person beyond your reach: not the *perfect* you. When you choose to be who you are, and make enhancements that will improve your quality of life without grasping for something that is impossible, then—and only then—will you be happy living your life.

Acknowledging that there is room for improvement or even change in your life is the vital first step toward achieving balance and happiness. Take pride that you've taken that first step and take pride again for each step you take hereafter. I think of that trite saying that I used to find very annoying: You get what you pay for. It's true, though. Your outcome is usually in direct proportion to the amount you were willing to "pay" for it: in energy, in time, in work, and in thought.

There is no magic elixir for happiness and success. But there is a process that combines the technology of the mind with learning how to discover your own purpose. As long as the subject (that's you) is willing to do his or her part, the odds of achieving peak happiness and well being increase exponentially. Here are my final recommendations:

Follow and complete the Perfect Enough **DISCOVER PROCESS** program.

- Record your thoughts and feelings about taking responsibility for reaching your goals. In addition to monitoring whether you practiced, did your self-hypnosis sessions, and maintained a good attitude, you can respond to the following:

  1) The best part of my thought today was:
  2) My feelings during work today were:
  3) What I learned about me and my ability to be positive today was:
  4) I learned the following about myself today:
  5) I learned the following about my spouse/partner/child today:
  6) I learned the following about my life today:
  7) I am grateful for these things in my life today:

- I cannot emphasize enough that you should set standards and goals that are very specific. And that you establish points of progress to keep you in check. And that, above all, you should value your progress so much that you are brimming with pride from your achievements.

The buck stops with you. You owe it to yourself to avail yourself of all of your resources: your best friend, your spouse or special someone, and your entire mind and body. I wish you the best of life and I trust you will give yourself the gift of balance and happiness.

Smiling makes you feel good;
it stimulates chemicals in your brain that elevate your mood.
Smile more often!

YOU ARE WORTH IT!

REFERENCES

Borysenko, Joan. *Minding the Body, Mending the Mind.* Bantam: 1988.

Carlson, Richard. *You Can Be Happy No Matter What: Five Principles for Keeping Life in Perspective.* New World: 1997.

Dictionary.com. *American Heritage Dictionary.* (accessed: May 13, 2007).

Dictionary.com. *Dictionary.com Unabridged (v 1.0.1).* Random House, Inc. http://dictionary.reference.com/browse/elevating (accessed: December 16, 2006).

Dictionary.com. *Merriam-Webster's Medical Dictionary.* Merriam-Webster, Inc. http://dictionary.reference.com/browse/health (accessed: January 05, 2007).

Dictionary.com. *Dictionary.com Unabridged (v 1.0.1),* Based on the Random House Unabridged Dictionary, © Random House, Inc. 2006. http://dictionary.reference.com/browse/love (accessed: September 30, 2006).

Dictionary.com. *Dictionary.com Unabridged (v 1.0.1).* Random House, Inc. http://dictionary.reference.com/browse/persistent (accessed: December 7, 2006).

Dictionary.com. *Dictionary.com Unabridged (v 1.0.1)*, Based on the Random House Unabridged Dictionary, © Random House, Inc. 2006. http://dictionary.reference.com/browse/prosperity (accessed: September 30, 2006).

Dictionary.com. *Dictionary.com Unabridged (v 1.0.1)*. Random House, Inc. http://dictionary.reference.com/browse/purpose (accessed: December 13, 2006).

Dictionary.com. *Dictionary.com Unabridged (v 1.0.1)*. Random House, Inc. http://dictionary.reference.com/browse/selfish (accessed: December 16, 2006).

Dictionary.com. *The American Heritage® Dictionary of the English Language, Fourth Edition*, Houghton Mifflin Company, 2004. http://dictionary.reference.com/browse/vitality (accessed: September 30, 2006).

Dyer, Wayne. *Manifest Your Destiny*. Harper Collins: 1997.

Dyer, Wayne. *The Power of Intention*. Hay House: 2004.

Harris, Carol. *NLP Made Easy*. Element: 2003.

Hay, Louise. *You Can Heal Your Life*. Hay House: 1999.

Hill, Napoleon. *Keys to Success: The 17 Principles of Personal Achievement*. Plume: 1994.

Hill, Napoleon. *Think and Grow Rich*. Plume: 1990.

King, Laura. *The Power to Win*. Lyons: 2004.

Murphy, Joseph. *The Power of Your Subconscious Mind*. Bantam: 2001.

Ruiz, Don Miguel. *The Four Agreements Companion Book*. Amber Allen: 2000.

Tolle, Eckhart. *The Power of Now: A Guide to Spiritual Enlightenment*. New World: 1999.

Ziglar, Zig. *See You at the Top*. Pelican: 1990.

LIST OF OTHER PRODUCTS BY LAURA KING
GO TO WWW.LAURAKING.NET

BOOKS

The Power to Win
The Power to Win Companion Book
Awesome Golf Now
Perfect Enough   Perfect Enough Companion Book

MOTIVATIONAL CD'S WITH
SELF HYPNOSIS CD'S SERIES

Perfect Enough CD SET
MAXIMIZE YOUR DISCOVER PROCESS
Consious Level and Subconscious Level Processing
Includes 16 CD's plus bonus CD's

Key #1 - Self Confidence 2 CDs   Key #2 - Self-Talk 2 CDs
Key #3 - Persistence 2 CDs   Key #4 - Life & Aliveness 2 CDs
Key #5 - Health 2 CDs   Key #6 - Love 2 CDs
Key #7 - Prosperity 2 CDs   Key #8 - Meaning 2 CDs

SELF HYPNOSIS CD'S & SERIES

Complete Weight Loss/Be Fit for Life Series
Plus DVD   Also in Spanish

Healthy Eating for Weight Loss CD   Speeding up Your Metabolism CD
Ideal Body Image CD   Be Fit Mentally CD
Be Your Best CD   Courage to Let Go CD
Be Fit for Life Exercise DVD   Smart Health for Life CD
Companion Workbook - Complete Weight Loss
Motivation to Exercise CD **Bonus** Motivation to Be Fit Screen Saver

SMART HEALTH FOR LIFE SERIES * 3 CD SET

Letting Go of ED (Eating Disorders) Series
Desire To Be Healthy CD   Healthy Eating for Body & Soul CD

Stop Now – Release ED CD

Additional Smart Health for Life CDs

Relief for IBS CD

Stop Drinking Be Healthy CD

Healthy Lifestyle Choices for IBS CD

Stop Smoking CD

Empower Your Holiday Spirit CD

PERSONAL KEYS TO WINNING FOR LIFE SERIES

Basic Relaxation CD

Exercise CD

Letting Go / Moving Forward CD

Health CD

Healthy Choices / Ideal Weight CD

Feel Good / Be Happy CD

Quiet Sleeper, Stop Snoring CD

Stop Nail Biting CD

Remembering Names CD

RELATIONSHIPS FOR LIFE SERIES

Improve Your Sex Drive CD

Relaxation to Get Pregnant CD

Relax to Get Pregnant In-Vitro CD

Relax to Stay Pregnant CD

Balance For Your Relationships CD

Attract the Ideal Husband CD

The Diplomatic Wife CD

The Diplomatic Partner CD

The Diplomatic Parent CD

Do It All CD

LEARN SERIES

Concentration CD

Absorption CD

Excellent Thinker CD

Recall CD

Test Taking / Good Study Habits CD

Alert CD

Standardized Test Taking CD

Conscious Student CD

CORPORATE / BUSINESS SERIES

Public Speaking CD

Building Sales CD

Motivation CD

Stress Management CD

Increase Your Memory CD

Prosperity / Abundance CD

Winning Job Interviews CD

Remember Names CD

COMPLETE WELLNESS SERIES

Preparing Your Mind for Surgery CD
Maximize Your Treatment Potential CD
Improving Your Immune System CD
Comfort Management CD
Positive Emotional Management CD
Sleep Wonderfully CD

WORKING THROUGH GRIEF
& REGAINING HAPPINESS SERIES

* 2 CD Set

Grieving CD   Feel Good / Be Happy CD

ACHIEVING FLAWLESS AUDITIONS
& PERFORMANCES SERIES

* 2 CD Set

Improve Memory and Increase Concentration CD
Release Performance Anxiety CD

PLEASANT JOURNEYS SERIES

Fearless Flying CD   No More Seasickness CD
Let Go of Jetlag CD   Overcome Insomnia CD

CHILDREN

Stop Bedwetting CD   Weight Loss for Children CD
Overcoming WOW – Gaming Addiction CD   Stop Nail Biting CD

SPORTS

Improve Athletic Performance CD   Run Faster / Run Longer CD
Improve Your Tennis Game CD   Improve Your Baseball Skills CD
Improve Your Billiard Skills CD

Improve Your Motorcross Racing Skills CD
Improve Your Swimming Skills CD

KEYS TO WINNING FOR THE EQUESTRIAN SERIES

Also in Spanish
Basic Relaxation for the Equestrian CD
Fearless Showing and Jumping CD
Peak Performance- Building Confidence, Poise, and Self-Image CD
Release of Performance Anxiety CD
Gaining Concentration for the Equestrian CD
Positive Self Talk for the Equestrian CD

KEYS TO WINNING FOR THE WESTERN RIDER SERIES

Basic Relaxation CD   Fearless Showing CD
Release of Performance Anxiety CD   Peak Performance CD
Gaining Concentration and Memory CD Positive Self Talk CD

KEYS TO WINNING FOR THE JUMPER SERIES

Also in Spanish
Peak Performance CD   Conquering Fear CD
Gaining Concentration and Memory CD

KEYS TO WINNING FOR 3-DAY EVENTING SERIES

Peak Performance CD   Conquering Fear CD
Gaining Concentration and Memory CD

KEYS TO WINNING DRESSAGE SERIES

Also in Spanish
Peak Performance CD   Freestyle Relaxation to Dance CD
Gaining Concentration and Memory CD

AWESOME GOLF NOW! SERIES

Calm, Cool & Collected CD

Gaining Concentration CD

Mastering Fear CD

Positive Self-Talk CD

Release of Performance Anxiety CD

Achieving Peak Performance CD

FLAWLESS DOG SHOWING SERIES

Basic Relaxation for the Handler CD   Fearless Showing CD

Peak Performance - Building Confidence, Poise, and Self Image CD

Release of Performance Anxiety CD

Gaining Concentration for the Handler CD

Positive Self-Talk for the Dog Handler CD

AWESOME CHEERLEADING SERIES

Basic Relaxation for the Cheerleader CD   Fearless Cheering CD

Peak Performance - Building Confidence, Poise, and Self-Image CD

Release Performance Anxiety CD

Gaining Concentration for the Cheerleader CD

Positive Self-Talk for the Cheerleader CD

INDIVIDUAL CDS

Personalized Self-Hypnosis Session CD

Overcome Insomnia CD

Power CD

RECOMMENDED LEARNING RESOURCES

Calvin Banyan   www.hypnosiscenter.com

Banyan Hypnosis Center for Training & Services, Tustin, CA

Robert Brenner   www.brennerhypnosis.com

Brenner Hypnosis, Deland, FL

Shawn Brookhouse   www.ShaunBrookhouse.org

Brookhouse Hypnotherapy, Ltd, Manchester/ London

Beryl Comar   www.comarfowler.com

The CHANGE Associates, Dubai, United Arab Emirates

Michelle Drum-Matteson
The Mind and Body Spa, Charleston, IL

Elsom Eldridge   www.obvious-expert.com
The Obvious Expert, Winter Springs, FL

Ron Eslinger   www.elsinger.net
Healthy Visions Wellness Center, Oak Ridge, TN

Wendi Friesen   www.wendi.com
Wendi.com, El Dorado Hills, CA

Rev. C. Scot Giles   www.csgiles.org
Rev. C. Scot Giles, Dim., LLC, Wheaton, IL

C. Devin Hastings   www.mindbodyhypnosis.com
Mind Body Hypnosis, Minnetonka, MN

Kevin Hogan   www.KevinHogan.com
Kevin Hogan.com – The Resource Center, Eagan, MN

Dr. Lisa Halpin   www.hypnosisdoctor.com
HypnoCoach Training, San Ramon, CA

Dr. William Horton   www.nfnlp.com
National Federation of NeuroLinguistic Programming, Englewood, FL

Gerald F. Kein   www.omnihypnosis.com
Omni Hypnosis Training Center, Deland, FL

Don Mottin   www.donmottin.com
Mottin & Johnson Institute of Hypnosis, Bridgeton, MO

Marie Mongan   www.hypnobirthing.com
Hypno Birthing The Mongan Method, Pembroke, NH

Scott McFall   www.hypnosisconnection.com
McFall Publishing, Inc., Bismarck, ND

Thomas Nicoli   www.tomnicoli.com
A Better You Hypnosis, Woburn, MA

Bob Reese   www.reeseresolution.com
Reese Resolution Services, Roanoke, VA

Richard Sutphen   www.richardsutphen.com
Valley of The Sun Publishingl, Malibu, CA

INDEX

Affirmations, 16, 80, 127, 131-133, 199
Alpha conditioning
  concentration, 21, 24, 36, 52, 93,
    102, 150, 251-254
  fear, 33, 40, 48-49, 70-71, 87,
    89-90, 93, 100-104, 123, 143,
    145, 156, 161, 164, 177, 179-180,
    196-197, 205-206, 211, 213,
    228-229, 253-254
  performance, 24-25, 54, 103, 123,
    145-146, 166-167, 252-254
  relaxation, 12, 14, 20, 22, 30, 33,
    43, 51-58, 60, 103, 113, 115-116,
    138, 154-155, 159, 170-171, 179,
    184-185, 189, 191-192, 203-204,
    206, 221-222, 238, 251, 253-254
alpha state, 27, 54-55, 59-60, 113, 131,
    138, 154, 170, 189, 204, 221, 238
analytical mind, 32
anchoring, 74, 78, 166
anger, 9, 43, 48, 71, 90, 95, 133
animal magnetism, 23
attitude
  choice and, 208, 241
  effects of, 14, 24, 61
  of gratitude, 84, 96-97, 134, 164,
    174, 218, 226
  reactions and, 67, 225
authority figures, 48

Bandler, Richard, 64
body functions, 31, 35, 90, 192
Braid, James, 24
brain
  alpha state, 27, 54-55, 59-60, 113,
    131, 138, 154, 170, 189, 204, 221,
    238
  mind, 4-5, 12-15, 21-22, 25,
    27, 30-47, 49-53, 55, 58-60, 62,
    65, 71-72, 74-78, 82-83, 85-89,
    91, 93-94, 96, 101-109, 111-117,
    119-120, 124, 126, 131, 133-134,
    137-141, 145, 147, 151, 153-159,

164-167, 170-172, 174, 176-179,
    183-195, 199-200, 204-206,
    208-209, 211, 217, 220-224, 226,
    230, 234, 238, 241, 244-245,
    247-248, 252
  theta state, 27
breathing, 35, 71-72, 133, 166, 190-191

cause and effect, 75, 83
Circle of Excellence, 74-75
color, 36, 77, 119, 132, 140, 195, 215,
    223
communication, 65, 67, 69, 200, 225
compounding, 61, 214
concentration, 21, 24, 36, 52, 93, 102,
    150, 251-254
confidence, 55, 74-75, 100, 104-106,
    110-112, 116-118, 122, 139-140,
    143, 145, 149, 152, 158, 170-174,
    197, 202, 219, 250, 253-254
conscious mind
  critical factor, 45-48, 51
  functions of, 37, 82, 90, 192
  mental-conditioning laws, 72
  properties of, 27, 44, 177, 184,
    193
  subconscious and, 12, 25, 30, 35,
    37, 39, 41, 43-45, 49-50, 87, 89,
    93, 131-132, 136, 183, 234, 237,
    250
critical factor, 45-48, 51

danger, 40, 101, 120, 165
daydreams, 39
DISCOVER PROCESS
  Self-Confidence, 5, 15, 62, 70, 100,
    104-105, 109-112, 115-119, 215,
    225
  Self-Talk, 5, 15, 62, 120-124,
    129-130, 133-140, 146, 150, 156,
    250, 254
  Persistence, 5, 15, 62, 142-143,
    146, 148, 150-158, 225, 250

Life and Aliveness, 5, 15, 75, 160,
168-172
Health, 5, 15, 24, 41, 54, 62, 70,
93, 95, 122, 139, 176-182, 184,
186-195, 214, 220, 241, 247, 250-
251
Love, 3, 5, 10, 15, 22, 48, 62, 70,
72, 85, 97, 104-107, 115-116,
118, 128, 161, 170-171, 173-174,
180-181, 192-194, 196-204,
206-209, 214, 218, 222, 224-225,
231, 233, 241-242, 247, 250
Prosperity
Meaning, 5, 15, 62, 66, 69, 83,
104, 162, 172-173, 199, 228-229,
231-239, 241, 250
disgust, 72
dreams, 29, 39, 58, 134, 212, 220, 240
Dyer, Wayne, 85, 89, 97, 210, 248

Elman, Dave, 20, 26, 45
emotions
communications, 2, 10
management, 24, 187, 252
energy, 35-36, 40, 50, 71, 82-84, 92,
110, 116-118, 122, 124, 132, 134,
155, 160, 163, 171-174, 177-178,
182-184, 186, 190-191, 193-194,
198, 209, 217, 225-226, 235, 238-
239, 244
Erickson, Milton H., 24
Eternal present, 86

fantasies, 39
fear
definition, 4, 67, 123, 148, 214,
228
examples, 71, 121, 133, 200
exercises, 77, 102
irrational, 40, 102
scripts, 59, 76, 78, 80
feedback, 68
frequency of impression, 93
frequently asked questions
hypnosis
Neuro-Linguistic Programming ,
5, 13, 15, 25-26, 62, 64-65, 67, 78

Gates, Dorothy, 26, 82, 92, 107, 134
goals
challenges

success, 8, 34, 64-66, 68, 73, 75,
77, 91, 93, 117-118, 133, 136, 143,
148, 150, 153, 157-159, 186, 210,
214, 223-226, 234, 244, 248
gratitude, 84, 96-97, 134, 164, 174,
218, 226
Grinder, John, 64

habits, 12, 19, 34, 38, 46, 73, 91-93,
96, 140, 150, 152, 178, 186-187,
220, 251
healing, 25, 30, 177, 179, 181-182,
184, 186, 191, 193-194
Health, 5, 15, 24, 41, 54, 62, 70, 93,
95, 122, 139, 176-182, 184, 186-
195, 214, 220, 241, 247, 250-251
Hill, Napoleon, 93, 141, 248
human relations, 85
hypnosis
attitude, 49-51, 54, 84, 94-97, 109,
118, 140, 146, 164, 174, 218, 245
critical factor, 45-48, 51
fears and phobias, 49
history, 19, 22, 64, 179, 236
modern, 24, 26
waking, 35, 48, 54, 58, 115

ideas, 60, 77, 96, 113, 138, 154, 171,
185, 189, 204, 220, 222-223, 225,
238
images, 14, 16, 19, 39, 41-42, 75, 89,
91, 101, 107-108, 111-112, 132,
136, 153, 169, 179, 185, 188, 202,
215, 220, 236, 239
imagination, 34, 39-41, 76-77, 91, 101,
115, 156, 167, 173, 190, 205-206,
216, 224
information processing
auditory, 42, 79, 185
kinesthetic, 79-80
visual, 42, 79, 178, 185

King, Joan, 147
language, 25, 44, 65, 71, 79, 121, 125,
127, 130-131, 136, 149, 176, 178,
181-182, 201-202, 215, 235, 248

laws of the universe
cause and effect, 75, 83
change, 10-14, 19, 21-22, 25, 34,
37, 39, 43, 45-46, 49-51, 65-66,

68, 70-71, 81, 83, 87-94, 96, 103-
104, 109-110, 115, 117, 122, 124,
130-131, 135, 139, 143-145, 147-
148, 150, 162-164, 168, 183, 186,
209, 215, 229, 232, 234, 244
free thought, 84
human relations, 85
perception, 30, 40, 45, 69, 77, 86
work, 8, 15, 20, 26, 34-35, 40-41,
43, 49-51, 53-54, 59, 61, 64-65,
68-69, 75, 85, 88, 90, 92, 107,
109, 116, 119, 121-122, 124, 126,
129, 131-132, 137, 139-140, 143-
145, 148-149, 151-153, 159, 161,
166, 174, 181-182, 184, 195, 199,
206, 208-210, 215, 223, 225, 227-
229, 231-234, 237, 242, 244-245
life experience, 40-42, 163-164, 199,
234
Life and Aliveness, 5, 15, 75, 160,
168-172
Love, 3, 5, 10, 15, 22, 48, 62, 70, 72,
85, 97, 104-107, 115-116, 118,
128, 161, 170-171, 173-174, 180-
181, 192-194, 196-204, 206-209,
214, 218, 222, 224-225, 231, 233,
241-242, 247, 250

Meaning, 5, 15, 62, 66, 69, 83, 104,
162, 172-173, 199, 228-229,
231-239, 241, 250
meditation, 21, 184-185
memory
conscious mind, 13, 22, 30-36,
42, 44-47, 52, 58, 72, 78, 96, 111,
139, 179, 220
exercise, 16, 43, 92, 102-103, 166,
169, 179, 183-184, 187, 190, 230,
232, 235, 251
subconscious, 12-14, 16, 22,
25, 30, 33-52, 55, 58, 60-61, 75,
86-89, 91-93, 101, 105-108, 111,
113-114, 119, 124-127, 130-134,
136-139, 150-151, 155-156, 158,
165-166, 170-171, 177-179, 183,
188-189, 191, 194-195, 199-200,
203-205, 215, 220-222, 229, 234,
237-238, 248, 250
mistakes, 12, 67, 84, 101, 104, 110,
121-122, 143-147, 149-150, 180,
197

modeling, 16, 74, 109-110, 135-136,
152, 168-169, 187, 201, 219,
235-236

Natural Laws of the Mind, 5, 13, 15,
62, 82, 88
negative thinking, 29, 129, 140
Neuro-Linguistic Programming
practice, 15, 52-53, 55, 59, 66, 73,
76-77, 106, 124, 139, 144, 166,
179, 185, 218, 220, 225
principles of, 48, 68, 93, 248
techniques, 10, 39, 42, 49, 65-67,
73, 151

outcomes, 14, 67, 69, 111, 119, 136,
139, 144, 157-158, 220, 223-225

patience, 148, 197
perception
attitude, 49-51, 54, 84, 94-97, 109,
118, 140, 146, 164, 174, 218, 245
law of, 83-88, 91, 118, 182, 197,
199, 213, 217, 222, 224
Perfect Enough Toolkit, 16
Persistence, 5, 15, 62, 142-143, 146,
148, 150-158, 225, 250
perfection, 13, 122-123, 146-147, 167,
229
performance
alpha conditioning
confidence, 55, 74-75, 100,
104-106, 110-112, 116-118, 122,
139-140, 143, 145, 149, 152, 158,
170-174, 197, 202, 219, 250, 253-
254
Perls, Fritz, 64
phobias, 40, 49
plasticity, 93
positive thinking, 139
practice, 15, 52-53, 55, 59, 66, 73, 76-
77, 106, 124, 139, 144, 166, 179,
185, 218, 220, 225
present, 69, 74, 86, 121, 132, 148-150,
162, 166, 178, 198, 223, 230
Prosperity, 5, 15-16, 62, 70, 210-211,
214-215, 217, 219-222, 224-226,
248, 250, 252
reactions, 67, 94-95, 125, 127, 163,
225, 231
reasoning, 22, 28, 33

relaxation
    alpha state, 27, 54-55, 59-60, 113,
    131, 138, 154, 170, 189, 204, 221,
    238
    basic, 52, 197, 211, 213, 251, 253-
    254
    compounding, 61, 214
    examples, 71, 121, 133, 200
    exercises, 77, 102
    scripts, 59, 76, 78, 80
    self-hypnosis, 13, 20, 22, 26-27,
    30, 51-53, 59, 78-80, 112, 131,
    137, 153, 166, 185, 188, 220,
    237, 245, 255

Satir, Virginia, 64
scripts, 59, 76, 78, 80
Self-Confidence, 5, 15, 62, 70, 100,
    104-105, 109-112, 115-119, 215,
    225
self-hypnosis
    alpha state, 27, 54-55, 59-60, 113,
    131, 138, 154, 170, 189, 204, 221,
    238
basic relaxation
    compounding, 61, 214
    rules for, 52
    self-talk, 5, 15, 62, 120-124, 129-
    130, 133-140, 146, 150, 156, 250,
    254
Self-inquiry, 16
self-knowledge, 78
self-talk
    alpha state, 27, 54-55, 59-60, 113,
    131, 138, 154, 170, 189, 204, 221,
    238
    changing, 22, 33-34, 49, 71, 88,
    96, 110, 124, 130, 144, 185, 209,
    232
    definition, 4, 67, 123, 148, 214,
    228
    examples, 71, 121, 133, 200
    improvement of, 85, 135
    positive, 12, 14, 19, 22, 25, 39,
    46, 49-50, 60, 66-67, 70, 83, 92,
    94, 97, 102, 106, 109, 112-118,
    122-124, 127-132, 134-140, 144,
    147, 154, 157, 163-164, 166-167,
    171, 177, 179, 182-184, 189, 193,
    199-200, 204, 209, 216, 221-223,
    226, 236, 238-241, 245, 252-254

release and clear, 87, 112-113, 115,
    156, 205
    scripts, 59, 76, 78, 80
    words to avoid, 125
state of mind, 47, 51, 145
subconscious mind
    conscious mind, 13, 22, 30-36,
    42, 44-47, 52, 58, 72, 78, 96, 111,
    139, 179, 220
    memory exercise, 43
    properties, 27, 44, 177, 184, 191,
    193

television, 47, 106, 108
tension, 29, 51-52, 54, 56-58, 80, 93,
    103, 113, 133, 166, 192, 208
Theater of the Mind, 74, 76-77, 103
theta state, 27
thoughts, 12-13, 15, 33, 39, 42, 45, 51,
    64-65, 68-69, 74-75, 83-84, 86-93,
    96, 106, 112, 115-118, 120-122,
    124, 136-137, 139, 150, 156-157,
    159, 164, 166-167, 176-178, 180-
    185, 187, 192-195, 198, 201-202,
    206, 216, 220, 225, 235-236,
    239-241, 245

unconscious incompetence, 73

visualization, 14, 76, 132

waking hypnosis, 48
willpower, 31, 34, 36, 41, 150
work, 8, 15, 20, 26, 34-35, 40-41, 43,
    49-51, 53-54, 59, 61, 64-65, 68-
    69, 75, 85, 88, 90, 92, 107, 109,
    116, 119, 121-122, 124, 126, 129,
    131-132, 137, 139-140, 143-145,
    148-149, 151-153, 159, 161, 166,
    174, 181-182, 184, 195, 199, 206,
    208-210, 215, 223, 225, 227-229,
    231-234, 237, 242, 244-245
working memory, 31, 34

zone, the, 165